PharmaSim:
A Brand Management Simulation

Stuart W. James, Interpretive Software
Thomas C. Kinnear, The University of Michigan
Michael Deighan, Interpretive Software

Interpretive Software, Inc.
Charlottesville, Virginia

For more information about other products from Interpretive Software, please contact:

Interpretive Software, Inc.
1932 Arlington Blvd., Suite 107
Charlottesville, VA 22903
Phone: (804) 979-0245
Fax: (804) 979-2454
EMail: pharmasim@interpretive.com
Website: http://www.interpretive.com

TABLE OF CONTENTS

ACKNOWLEDGMENTS

The authors wish to thank many people for their support in the development of this simulation. Mary Juraco and Kathleen Simroth of Interpretive Software were a great help with the editing process for the initial version of this manual. Melissa Rosati, Jim Boyd and Jim Sitlington at Scott, Foresman and Company all played an important role in getting PharmaSim off the ground. Steve and Kathleen Simroth and Karen James collected data in retail outlets long before the first line of code was written. We also are grateful to the many students who tested all the versions of PharmaSim over its development. A special thanks is due Eric Anderson, Craig Ehrnst, Matt Hausmann, Nadine Lindley, Jim Pack, Louise Bedard and Joanne Novak at the University of Michigan Business School for their help in the alpha and beta test phases of PharmaSim. Julie Koh suggested a number of key improvements for the user interface in version 2. Gabriel Buddenbrock helped edit the latest version of the manual. Anne Smith at HarperCollins coordinated faculty reviews of the previous version and helped make this new release of PharmaSim a reality.

The latest releases of PharmaSim have benefited greatly from the input of Jose Rosa of the University of Illinois, Ann Root, Gene Anderson of the University of Michigan, and Lori Feldman and Hugh Daubek of Purdue University at Calumet. We also appreciate being invited into the classrooms and meetings by the first year marketing faculty at the Harvard and Darden Business Schools. We consider all customers part of our product development team, and we are fortunate they have put their time and effort into improving our product. We especially appreciate the suggestions and comments of the many faculty who have used PharmaSim over the years.

This manual was printed by Kaminer and Thomson of Charlottesville, Virginia. Cover design by Luis Muench.

This simulation is dedicated to Karen and Katherine,
Connie, Maggie, and Jamie,
Mary, Justin, Mikaela, Kathleen, and Sean.

Introduction

Computer based simulations are becoming an increasingly popular and useful tool for learning and applying business concepts. For students, simulations offer the opportunity to experience much of the realism of making business decisions in the classroom. Managers and other executives can use simulations to sharpen their strategy formulation skills or learn about the dynamics of different industries. The average individual may use the simulation to explore unfamiliar territory in a forgiving environment.

PharmaSim is a computer simulation based on the over-the-counter (OTC) cold medicine industry. The exercise focuses primarily on marketing activities and is designed to teach marketing concepts in an active and stimulating environment. As a member of a marketing management team, you will make decisions regarding product mix, pricing, distribution, advertising, and promotion. These decisions will then be incorporated into a computer simulated market to reveal how both you and your competition performed. Decisions cover a time-span of 10 simulated years, allowing you to observe both the short-term and long-term effects of your decisions.

Competing in the PharmaSim market place will require complex analysis and decision making. Therefore, take some time to familiarize yourself with the program and manual before beginning the exercise. While working through the simulation, you will find it helpful to refer to the manual for information and strategy tips. In order to use the PharmaSim program most effectively, we recommend the following approach:

- *Read the PharmaSim Case*

  Section 1 of this manual presents a description of the market and your firm's current situation. A thorough understanding of your firm's case history will help you make better decisions.

- *Learn How to Operate the Program*

  Section 2 provides information on how to use the simulation software, as well as a detailed description of each menu option. In order to quickly learn the functions of the menu commands and become familiar with operating the program, it will be helpful to have access to a computer as you work through this section. After installing the software, you will need to choose a scenario and playing level. We generally recommend scenario 1, and the default playing level, which gradually increases decision responsibility over the ten periods.

  Note: At some universities, a customized version of PharmaSim will be used where scenario choice is not necessary.

- *Use the Reports to Analyze the Current Situation*

    Marketing research is available on-line from pull-down menus in the simulation. If you are using scenario 1, 2, or 3, the information in section 2 of your manual will match what is available in the software. Therefore, for your first decision, you will not need to buy marketing research. After the first decision, though, the information will be out of date and potentially unreliable.

    This research can provide key information about customer needs and buying behavior, consumer perceptions of your product, potential target markets, and comparative analyses of competing brands. From this information, you will devise and implement an appropriate long-term strategy. Just as in real-life, however, some information and reports will prove more useful than others. Part of your decision process will include deciding which information to purchase each period. These reports, located under the MARKET and SURVEY menus, along with the internal company reports under COMPANY, will help you analyze your current situation and the competitive environment. See section 3 for help in asking the right questions, finding the right data, and learning helpful hints.

    You may find it useful to print out some reports and step back from the computer from time to time. Analyzing information and determining an integrated marketing plan is a complex task. It is important to take time and reflect on the information, especially when working in groups.

- *Make Decisions*

    After reviewing information about your company, the competition, and the market, you will decide how to manage your brand in terms of product mix, price, sales force, promotion, and advertising. Sections 3 and 4 of the manual provide hints for structuring the decision process, including tips on situation analysis, strategy formulation, and alternative tactics. These chapters will provide a helpful guide to assimilating the large amount of information available. The Appendix contains decision and planning forms and technical information which you may also find helpful. Once you have made your marketing decisions, you will enter them into the computer under the DECISIONS menu.

    Consider the amount of time necessary to analyze the information and make decisions. This process requires an average of 1 1/2 hours, although one should allow extra time for the first to get acclimated to the simulation. Make sure you allow sufficient time to thoroughly analyze your resources and make well-planned decisions. This is especially important in the periods when you launch new products or line extensions.

- *What if...*

    Use the WHAT IF... option in the DECISIONS menu to run a financial check on your input decisions. This option will not forecast sales based on your decisions, but it can be used to experiment with different sales and pricing assumptions.

    If you find your company having financial difficulties as the simulation progresses, it might prove helpful to study Key Problems, located in Section 3 of the manual. An index and glossary have also been provided for your convenience for more information on specific issues.

- *Advance to the Next Period*

  After your decisions are entered, use the FILE pull-down menu and select ADVANCE TO NEXT PERIOD. The computer will then process your decisions and advance the simulation to the next year.

- *Review Results*

  Review the results in the market before making decisions for the next year. The simulation does not specifically tell which strategies worked and which did not. Instead, you must compare your results with those of your competition and consider how well your strategy is working. You may find some of the comparative graphs helpful in your analysis.

- *Repeat*

  Repeat the decision making process until all 10 periods have been completed. At the end of the simulation, you will be able to see how your brands performed over a 10 year span.

As you work through the simulation and become familiar with the program, new issues and problems will arise to challenge you. These will include reformulating your product and introducing new brands. Along with having to manage new brands, you will also be given more control over marketing mix decisions as the game progresses. You will cover issues such as targeting advertising and consumer promotion to particular customer segments, offering trade promotion and sales force to different distribution channels, and using volume pricing discounts.

Of course, the competition will be following their own strategies and reacting to your decisions. Although the simulation always starts from the same position, each game will proceed on a unique course depending on the strategy that each player chooses. This will allow competitive comparisons and illustrate how markets can evolve differently.

Using PharmaSim should be an exciting and rewarding experience. From the exercise, you will gain a practical understanding of marketing components and how various factors interact and affect one another. By analyzing information, making decisions, and observing the results, you will experience first hand the challenges and rewards of marketing.

The PharmaSim Manual

The remainder of this manual is divided into five sections:

1.   The PharmaSim Case

     This section presents the OTC cold medicine industry in a form similar to a business school case. It will also serve as an introduction to the situation when starting the simulation.

     Note: The exhibits in the case may not match reports taken from the simulation software. The values in the case and exhibits only match scenarios 1-3. Other scenarios may be similar, but one should rely only on the values in the software. Also, the level of detail of some of the information in the exhibits may not be applicable to the Brand Assistant's decisions (level 1).

2.   PharmaSim Operations Guide

     The guide outlines the operational aspects of using PharmaSim on the computer, including hardware requirements, installation of the software, interaction with the program, and a detailed description of each menu option. This section also describes the different playing levels and other options available in the software.

3.   Strategy and Tactics

     Section 3 discusses the use of situation analysis, strategy formulation, and alternative tactics. The processes described in this section will be critical throughout the simulation. Refer to it often!

4.   Resource Allocation Issues

     This section illustrates the use of portfolio analysis and introduces three resource allocation models currently used in business: The BCG growth share model, the cash sources / uses matrix, and the GE business position / industry attractiveness analysis.

5.   Appendix

     The last section of the manual provides you with decision and planning forms and technical information you may find useful. It also contains a glossary, index, and helpful trouble-shooting guide.

Section 1: The PharmaSim Case

ALLSTAR BRANDS' OTC COLD MEDICINE GROUP: THE ALLROUND BRAND

The management team at the over-the-counter cold medicine group (OCM) of Allstar Brands has just completed their third presentation in the past month to the pharmaceuticals division manager regarding the status of their Allround cold medication. It is apparent from all the attention the team has been receiving recently that the Allround brand they manage is of strategic importance to the company. Unfortunately for the team and the company, the fourth quarter performance reports for Allround were not as positive as management had expected. Therefore, for the last three weeks, the OCM team has been under the intense scrutiny of senior management.

Overview

Allstar Brands' Allround product is the current market share leader in the over-the-counter (OTC) cold and allergy remedy market. The consistent success of the brand in terms of both profitability and sales has made it extremely important to the pharmaceutical division's long term strategic plan. The division hopes that the brand's cash flow in the coming years will allow the company to pursue new opportunities in emerging markets. Recently, however, the division manager ultimately responsible for Allround has become concerned with the increasingly competitive nature of the OTC cold remedy market. In the past three years, the industry has seen several new product introductions as well as major increases in promotional and advertising expenditures. There is concern among senior management that this competitive activity will lead to declining market share and profitability for Allround. Already, the signs are apparent, as the brand has lost one full share point in the last year alone. Senior management expects that skillful marketing will be extremely important during the coming decade in order to insure the long-term success of Allstar Brands.

The Company

Allstar Brands Corporation is one of the leading manufacturers of packaged goods in the world. Since its founding in 1924, the company has bought or merged with a number of smaller packaged goods companies.

The company now consists of three divisions: Consumer Products, International, and Pharmaceuticals. Consumer Products handles a number of different packaged goods such as laundry detergent, shampoo, and bar soap. The International division distributes Allstar products on a global basis and has a large presence in the European market. The Pharmaceuticals Division is responsible for the marketing and production of both ethical and OTC medications. Ethical drugs are available through pharmacies with a physician's prescription whereas OTC remedies are widely distributed without the need for a prescription.

The management of Allstar's pharmaceutical division is made up of a number of market related groups, one of these being the Over-The-Counter Cold Medicine (OCM) group. This group is primarily concerned with the marketing activities of the Allround brand and any line extensions or new product introductions which might fall under the same category. An overview of the corporate structure of Allstar Brands is presented in Exhibit 1.1.

Exhibit 1.1: Allstar Brands Divisional Structure

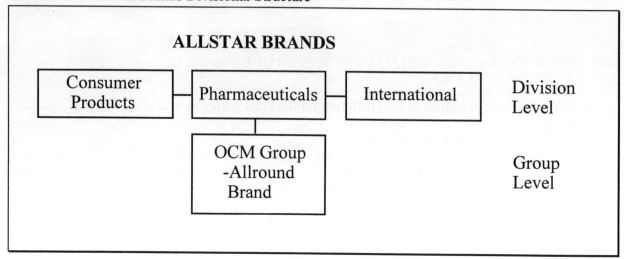

The Brand Management Group at OCM

The marketing management group responsible for Allround consists of a brand manager, an assistant brand manager, and a brand assistant who is a recent business school graduate. They work together as a team on all of the marketing decisions related to the OTC cold and allergy remedy market. Specifically, the three managers are concerned with developing the Allround marketing mix strategy each year, including any reformulation or line extension options. In addition, if Allstar's research department develops any promising new product ideas for the cold medicine market, this team will be responsible for the new product launch. Although all product and marketing decisions are made as a group, each member of the brand management team has a different functional role.

The brand assistant has major input on decisions related to retail price, promotional allowances, consumer and trade promotional expenditures, advertising expenditures, and the number of direct and indirect sales force personnel committed to the Allround brand. The brand manager thought it would be best for the brand assistant to gain experience by understanding the basic marketing variables before becoming more heavily involved in the detailed implementation of the marketing plan.

The assistant brand manager has input to the above issues as well, but is also required to make marketing decisions in much greater depth. For example, the assistant brand manager makes recommendations concerning the allocation of the sales force to end retailer types and across the direct and indirect channels. This person is also concerned with the development of the pricing discount structure, and more of the specifics of promotional programs including the advertising message used, the advertising agency selected, and the types of trade and consumer promotions used.

The brand manager is responsible for all aspects of the marketing decisions for the Allround brand. In addition to the decision areas above, the brand manager is uniquely responsible for more detailed aspects of the advertising message including which competitor to position against, the choice of target segments, and the details of how promotional allowances and promotions are allocated across the various channels of distribution.

In general, the brand management group is responsible for making effective marketing decisions in all marketing mix areas in order to maximize the long-term profitability of Allstar Brands' OTC cold and allergy remedy group.

Industry Overview

Allstar Brands competes with four other firms in the OTC cold and allergy market. These five firms offer a total of 10 brands in four different product categories as listed below in Exhibit 1.2:

Exhibit 1.2: Company and Brand Summary

Company Name	Sales (Millions)	Brands on the market
Allstar Brands	$355	"Allround", 4-hr cold liquid
B & B Health Care	$286	"Believe", 4-hr allergy capsule "Besthelp", 4-hr cold capsule
Curall Pharmaceuticals	$199	"Coughcure", 4-hr cough liquid
Driscol Corporation	$255	"Defogg", 4-hr allergy capsule "Dripstop", nasal spray "Dryup", 4-hr cold capsule
Ethik Incorporated	$395	"Effective", nasal spray "End", 4-hr cough liquid "Extra", 12-hr cold capsule

The OTC Cold Remedy Market

Cold remedies are designed to address five basic symptoms: 1) aches and fever, 2) nasal congestion, 3) chest congestion, 4) runny nose, and 5) cough. Though the cause is different, allergies share many of the same symptoms, and are therefore often grouped with cold remedies. However, products specifically formulated for allergy relief medicines are available, and it is common in the industry to consider relief from allergy symptoms as a separate consumer need from virus and flu related illnesses. Chronic allergy sufferers tend to have different usage patterns and more concerns about side effects because of the duration of the symptoms.

Brand Formulations

In general, OTC brands are formulated using various combinations of six basic types of ingredients. Each ingredient is targeted to address one of the symptoms listed above, or is used as a base for the other ingredients. The ingredients are as follows:

Analgesics:	Provide relief for aches and fever. Common analgesics are aspirin and acetaminophen (an aspirin substitute).
Decongestants:	Reduce nasal congestion by shrinking the blood vessels in the nose lining to clear the passages and restore free breathing.
Expectorants:	Provide relief from chest congestion by loosening the phlegm, thereby making each cough more efficient.
Antihistamines:	Reduce the secretions that cause runny nose and watery eyes.
Cough suppressants:	Reduce the cough reflex.
Alcohol:	Provides a base for the other ingredients in some products, and also helps the patient rest. Some consumers view alcohol as a negative attribute.

A brand can be made available in one of three forms: liquid, capsule, or spray. Although a consumer's choice with regard to form is usually based on personal preference, some general differences are apparent. Nasal sprays contain only a topical nasal decongestant that provides faster relief from sinus congestion than other forms. Capsule and liquid cold medications might contain any combination of ingredients, although cough medicine is usually found in liquid form to help soothe throat irritation. According to a recent survey, most consumers find that capsule form is somewhat more convenient than liquid. Exhibit 1.3 shows each of the current brand formulations on the market.

Two other basic product considerations are duration of the product and possible side effects. Product duration is typically either 4-hour or 12-hour. The Food and Drug Administration (FDA) regulates the amount of medication for various periods of relief, including the maximum for a 24 hour period without a prescription. The maximum dosage used in 4-hour formulations cannot be taken more than 4 times each day due to over-medication concerns. 12-hour formulations contain half the daily maximum medication. Nasal sprays are considered instant relief products because they act much faster than standard cold medicine. However, their effectiveness wears off faster as well. The duration for each brand on the market is listed in Exhibit 1.3.

Side effects have become a greater consideration in recent years because of the emphasis on healthier lifestyles and concerns about performance under medication. Drowsiness due to antihistamines or alcohol is the most often mentioned negative side effect, especially when these products are used during the day. However, other considerations include upset stomach, long-term effects of nasal spray, and providing excessive medication for the consumer's symptoms.

Exhibit 1.3: Current Brand Formulations

	Anal-gesic	Anti-hist	Dcngst	Cough Supp	Expect	Alcohol	
Max Allow	1000	4	60	30	200	20	(Mg/4 hr dose)
Allround	1000	4	60	30	0	20	4hr Multi Liquid
Believe	0	4	0	0	0	0	4hr Allergy Capsule
Besthelp	0	4	60	0	0	0	4hr Cold Capsule
Coughcure	0	0	30	30	0	10	4hr Cough Liquid
Defogg	0	4	0	0	0	0	4hr Allergy Capsule
Dripstop	0	0	60	0	0	0	Cold Spray
Dryup	1000	4	60	0	0	0	4hr Multi Capsule
Effective	0	0	60	0	0	0	Cold Spray
End	0	0	0	0	200	10	4hr Cough Liquid
Extra	0	0	120	0	0	0	12hr Cold Capsule

As can be seen in the exhibit, the Allround brand is a 4-hour liquid cold medicine that provides multi-symptom relief. It contains an analgesic, an antihistamine, a decongestant, a cough suppressant, and alcohol. Typically, most consumers use this product for night-time relief because of the strength of the medication and because the alcohol and antihistamine help the patient rest. Allround is viewed as one of the most effective brands on the market at reducing multiple cold symptoms. However, consumer groups and some physicians sometimes attack the multi-symptom "shot-gun" approach as providing more medication than is needed in many circumstances.

Market Segmentation and the Market Survey

The trade typically segments the OTC cold and allergy market on the basis of how the brands are labeled. The four standard product categories in the OTC market are cold, cough, allergy, and nasal spray. The brand management group often uses the information presented in Exhibit 1.4 as a basis for determining the brand's direct competition, but also realizes that the report fails to take into account cross-usage of brands (e.g. using a cold medicine to relieve allergy symptoms).

Exhibit 1.4: Market Share by Product Category

	% Cold	% Cough	% Allergy	% Nasal	% Total
Mfr. Sales (M$)	879.7	366.4	126.1	119.1	1491.2
Growth	6.6%	3.2%	5.9%	4.5%	5.5%
Allround	40.4%	0.0%	0.0%	0.0%	23.8%
Believe	0.0%	0.0%	50.7%	0.0%	4.3%
Besthelp	25.2%	0.0%	0.0%	0.0%	14.9%
Coughcure	0.0%	54.3%	0.0%	0.0%	13.3%
Defogg	0.0%	0.0%	49.3%	0.0%	4.2%
Dripstop	0.0%	0.0%	0.0%	52.0%	4.2%
Dryup	14.9%	0.0%	0.0%	0.0%	8.8%
Effective	0.0%	0.0%	0.0%	48.0%	3.8%
End	0.0%	45.7%	0.0%	0.0%	11.2%
Extra	19.5%	0.0%	0.0%	0.0%	11.5%

A major marketing research firm offers a nationwide survey of OTC cold and allergy consumers. The market research firm claims that this survey provides a great deal more information on how cold and allergy products are used and perceived by consumers. The firm also suggests that demographic segmentation could reveal important information about the market. The survey data is provided with two segmentation options: 1) illness: cold, cough, and allergy; and 2) demographics: young singles, young families, mature families, empty nesters, and retired. The marketing research firm compiles this study every year.

Curious about possible new market insights, the OCM group obtained partial non-segmented results of the market survey on a "free to examine" trial basis. If the group finds the sample data informative, it may purchase the complete survey this year for a price of $100,000. The OTC cold and allergy market could then be analyzed based on any or all combinations of illness and demographics that the Allround brand group desires.

Survey Data

The consumer survey consists of the following reports: 1) market share based upon consumer brand purchases; 2) the purchase decision-making criteria used by consumers; 3) brand awareness, trial, and repurchase percentages; 4) brand satisfaction; 5) a comparison of intended versus actual purchases; 6) a comparison of brands based on consumers' perceptions of their ability to relieve symptoms; and 7) the tradeoff that consumers perceive between symptom relief and price. The sample data for awareness, trial, and repurchase is presented in Exhibit 1.5 below.

The survey results on Brands Purchased, Purchase Intentions, and Satisfaction are based on units sold. Brand Awareness, Decision Criteria, Brand Perception, and Tradeoffs are based on survey population. This distinction reflects multiple purchases from one survey respondent (usage rates). Appendix 5 contains a copy of the market survey questionnaire.

Exhibit 1.5: Market Survey - Brand Awareness, Trials and Repurchase

Brand	Brand Awareness	Brand Trials	Most Freq. Purchase	Conversion Ratio	Retention Ratio
Allround	74.1%	47.1%	21.8%	63.6%	46.3%
Believe	18.9%	9.2%	3.8%	48.5%	41.9%
Besthelp	56.6%	30.0%	13.0%	53.1%	43.2%
Coughcure	49.0%	29.0%	18.4%	59.1%	63.6%
Defogg	24.1%	13.0%	4.1%	53.9%	31.8%
Dripstop	20.2%	11.3%	3.6%	56.1%	31.4%
Dryup	23.2%	10.9%	7.2%	47.0%	65.6%
Effective	22.0%	12.0%	3.1%	54.5%	26.2%
End	46.9%	30.6%	15.6%	65.3%	50.8%
Extra	60.1%	31.8%	9.5%	52.8%	29.9%

The OCM group found this data insightful. They were pleased that Allround had the highest awareness of any brand. Currently, 74.1% of consumers surveyed mentioned the Allround brand without prompting, which is considered "unaided awareness". In addition, the Allround brand had the highest trial level and was the brand most frequently purchased. Allround's conversion ratio (the percent of those aware of a brand who have tried it) is currently 63.6%. The brand manager noted with some concern that their retention ratio (the percent of those who have tried the brand who now purchase it most often) was lower than several other brands; most notably the new Dryup brand. The OCM group wondered if this might be a signal of future problems. However, the brand assistant recalled that new brands and brands which fill very specific needs often have higher retention rates than brands which are mature or not highly targeted.

Other Marketing Research

In addition to the survey data, other information about the market is available. Market trade publications, similar to Exhibit 1.4, are free to the Allround brand group and provide the following data: industry outlook on population, market growth rate, inflation, wholesale/direct distribution, and symptoms reported by consumers. Other data concerning competition and distribution are also available at this time for a fee. These include: 1) a comparison of relevant operating statistics for each company; 2) competitive estimates of sales force allocation, advertising expenditures and message, and promotional programs; 3) studies of distribution regarding share of channel sales, pricing, consumer shopping habits, average shelf space, and physician and pharmacist recommendations. All of these reports are discussed in Section 2.

The Allround brand group believes that useful information is contained in these studies. However, they also know that they need to examine the trade-off between the cost of these studies and the information for decision-making that the studies will provide. They also need to recognize that all marketing research studies have some error in them.

Industry Competition

The OCM group constantly monitors competitive activity in a number of areas, including pricing and promotion allowances, advertising, consumer and trade promotion, and sales force allocation.

Pricing and Promotional Allowances

It is industry practice for manufacturers to suggest retail prices to retailers, although retailers ultimately set the price to consumers. Manufacturers commonly offer a "promotional allowance" of 10-20% of the MSRP to retailers, plus volume discounts of 15-40%. Allowances are necessary to gain retail distribution, to obtain desired shelf facings in retail outlets, and to gain retailer support for a brand in advertisements and promotions undertaken by the retailer. Allowances are usually discussed with retailers in conjunction with price levels, but are also considered to be a type of promotional expense. Thus, allowances appear on the marketing plan and the income statement for a brand as part of promotion. Exhibit 1.6 displays the current pricing policies for the Allround brand.

Exhibit 1.6: Price/Volume Discount Schedule for Allround ($)

Suggested Retail	5.29			
By Discount Schedule	Price	Units	Dollars	%Total
Direct				
<250	3.97	10.5	41.8	11.8%
<2500	3.70	35.4	131.2	36.9%
2500+	3.44	15.1	51.9	14.6%
Indirect/Wholesale	3.17	41.1	130.3	36.7%

Note: This information is only available at level 2 and above in the software.

The current manufacturer suggested retail price for Allround is $5.29, with an average allowance of 17.0% given to retailers, in addition to volume discounts. Both of these values are somewhat higher than industry average. However, the OCM group believes that Allround's sales have not suffered because of the higher price. In fact, the brand's effectiveness, high recognition, and level of loyalty have allowed it to maintain a price leadership role in the market. Exhibit 1.7 provides manufacturer's suggested retail prices for all brands in the market. A market research report that shows the average retail price by channel is also available for $20,000 this year.

Exhibit 1.7: Manufacturer's Suggested Retail Prices ($)

Allround	$ 5.29
Believe	4.39
Besthelp	4.89
Coughcure	5.49
Defogg	4.29
Dripstop	4.29
Dryup	5.09
Effective	4.39
End	5.29
Extra	4.49

Advertising

Advertising plays a major role in establishing brand awareness with consumers and in helping to shape consumers' perceptions of products. The Allround brand group must make three basic advertising decisions each year: 1) the amount of dollars allocated to the advertising budget; 2) the content of the advertising message; and 3) the choice of an advertising agency. Last year, $20 million dollars were spent on Allround's advertising campaign, primarily for commercials aired on network television. Competitive advertising budgets for last year ranged from $1 million for the Effective brand to $16 million for Coughcure.

There are four basic advertising message types that the Allround brand group considers potentially useful for Allround: 1) primary demand stimulation where the advertising message is heavily focused on increasing overall demand for OTC remedies, but also helps to increase Allround's unaided awareness; 2) a benefits approach where the symptomatic relief properties of Allround are stated; 3) a comparison approach where Allround is directly compared and positioned against another brand; and 4) a reminder advertising message to keep the Allround name high in top-of-the-mind recall for consumers with the objective of maintaining awareness and stimulating repurchase. The advertising message used in any year can be any combination of these types. Last year, Allround's advertising was 5 percent primary demand, 45 percent benefits, 45 percent comparison, and 5 percent reminder. The advertising message can also be targeted in terms of product use (cold, cough, or allergy) and demographics (young singles, young families, mature families, empty nesters, retired). This targeting provides guidance to the advertising agency for creative aspects of the ad design, and selection of specific media buys.

The Allround brand group is in the process of considering the selection of a new advertising agency. Currently, Allround's agency is Brewster, Maxwell and Wheeler (BMW). This agency is known for its high quality work but charges a full 15 percent commission on media advertising placements. There is some concern that BMW is costing the Allround brand too much and having an adverse impact on profits. The Allround brand group has received solicitation for the Allround advertising business from two other agencies. The first firm, Sully & Rodgers (S&R), has a reputation of providing mid-range quality work, but charges only 10 percent on media placement. The other potential new agency is Lester Loebol & Company (LLC), which charges only 5% on placement, one-third as much as BMW. However, their advertising campaigns are of significantly lesser quality. The argument was made that since the Allround name is well established, a decrease in the quality of advertising might not hurt the brand significantly. Potential cost savings could result in an increase in profits. However, the group is concerned that lower quality advertising might hurt their brand image.

Consumer and Trade Promotion

Consumer and trade promotion is a significant part of marketing in the OTC cold and allergy remedy market. The Allround brand spent $7 million on consumer and trade promotion last year (not including promotional allowances of 17.0%). As was the case in advertising, the OCM group believes that Allround has more promotional support than any other brand currently on the market.

Trade promotions include promotional allowances and cooperative advertising. Promotional allowances were discussed in the pricing section, and are basically an additional discount to the channel. Cooperative advertising provides incentives to the channel to feature a specific brand in their own advertising. Money is made available to retailers to pay for a portion of the retailer's advertising when the relevant brand is promoted. Currently, Allround has $1.4 million allocated for this purpose.

Consumer promotions include distribution of free trial size packages, coupons, and point-of-purchase displays. Trial sizes are special smaller packages of a brand that are available at a lower price or are distributed directly to consumers. Last year Allround chose not to use trial size packaging, but is reconsidering that option for the current year. As the name implies, trial packaging usually contains a smaller dosage of medicine and is provided to potential consumers for free. This promotion is used to attract new users to try the Allround brand.

Coupons distributed to consumers in special newspaper or magazine supplements, offer additional discounts off of the retail price when redeemed at the time of purchase. In the last year, $4.2 million was spent on coupon support of the Allround brand. This includes money spent on printing, inserts, and mailings.

Point-of-purchase vehicles are special displays such as retail sale racks, on-shelf advertisements, or end-of-aisle displays that promote a brand to the consumer in the retail store. The OCM group believes that these displays promote brand switching when the consumer is purchasing OTC products. Point-of-purchase money is paid to the retailer, but the promotion is directed at the end consumer. Last year, $1.4 million was spent on point-of-purchase displays for Allround.

The brand management team not only sets the appropriation for each of these promotional activities, but also allocates the promotional effort across the types of retail outlets in the various channels of distribution. The brand manager may allocate these depending on factors such as shopping habits and channel needs. Exhibit 1.8 provides a summary of last year's promotional activity for the Allround brand.

Exhibit 1.8: Promotional Activity for the Allround Brand (in $000s)

Promo Allowances	$ 60,400	(17.0%)
Co-op Advert	1,400	
Point of Purchase	1,400	
Trial Size	0	
Coupons	4,200	($ .50 / ea)

Sales Force

The support of a manufacturer's sales force is critical to the success of a brand in the OTC cold and allergy market. Part of the sales force sells directly to retail outlets. This direct sales force is responsible for maintaining relationships with current retailers and for developing new retail accounts. Also, the direct sales force presents trade promotions, allowances, and new product introductions to retailers.

Manufacturers also maintain an indirect sales force designed to sell into and support the indirect distribution system in three ways. First, part of the indirect sales force, called the wholesale sales force, sells to and supports the selling activities of wholesalers. These wholesalers sell OTC brands to smaller, independent retailers that are not reached by the direct sales force of the manufacturer. Second, part of the indirect sales force, called the merchandisers, provides special support to retailers for their in-store activities such as shelf location, pricing, and compliance with special promotions. The third part of the indirect sales force, known as detailers, call on doctors and pharmacists to provide information about their brand and to introduce new products. The objective is to have the doctor or pharmacist recommend their brand to the end consumer.

The brand management team is fully responsible for the OCM sales force. Therefore, the team determines the total size of the sales force, including the proportion for direct and indirect support. In addition, the brand manager allocates the direct sales force to each type of retail outlet and the indirect sales force to its three components: wholesale sales force, merchandisers, and detailers. The team also has to be concerned with sales force hiring and training costs. The latter is especially important in the pharmaceutical business, even in OTC drugs. The Allround brand currently has a sales force of 127, resulting in a total cost of $6 million for salaries, expenses, and training. Sales force allocation for Allstar Brands is listed in Exhibit 1.9.

Exhibit 1.9: Allstar Brands - Sales Force Allocation

Direct	#SF
Indep Drugstores	6
Chain Drugstores	28
Grocery Stores	43
Convenience Stores	3
Mass Merch	14
Total Direct	94
Indirect	
Wholesaler Support	15
Merchandisers	8
Detailers	10
Total Sales Force	127

Channel Choices

OTC cold and allergy remedies are sold at retail in independent and chain drug stores, full-line grocery stores, convenience stores or small roadside markets such as 7-11, and mass merchandisers such as K mart. As noted above in the sales force discussion, Allround uses both direct and indirect channels of distribution. Generally, direct sales are to larger urban and suburban stores, and chain retail accounts. Wholesalers typically serve smaller retail outlets and more rural areas, where the revenues generated for Allround do not support the cost of maintaining a salesperson. The wholesaler carries many product lines and therefore has a broader revenue base for supporting the cost of their sales force.

Gaining the support of the channel is an extremely important part of a brand's success. As mentioned previously, shelf space allocation can have a significant effect on brand sales. The OCM group recently paid for a study of average shelf space in retail channels and found that Allround received the third best placement in the market. The group wondered why Allround did not receive the best placement, since the brand typically generated higher volume than any other OTC medication. Due to this concern, they asked their sales force to ask retailers how shelf space was allocated among brands. The results from this informal survey showed that there were four basic factors which the retailers considered: product turnover (how many units are sold in a given period of time), promotional allowances, sales force support, and co-op advertising allowances. In general, large grocery stores, mass merchandisers, and chain drug stores were more apt to focus only on turnover and allowances, whereas independent drugstores paid greater attention to sales force support. The OCM group hoped that this information might prove useful in determining how to allocate their resources across channels of distribution.

Internal Product Development

The Allround brand group is aware that it has important product development and management decisions to make over the next decade and works closely with the product research and development area (R&D) within Allstar Brands. R&D can provide three major types of product development for the Allround brand group: 1) reformulation of the ingredients in Allround; 2) line extensions of the basic Allround brand; and 3) development of a completely a new brand. New brand options may include ingredients currently available by prescription only should FDA regulations change. These proprietary prescription only medications may offer Allstar competitive advantages in the OTC market. After lengthy discussion, the OCM group and R&D have agreed that the following schedule will form the basis of the Allround brand group's product development decisions. After the given period of time these product alternatives would not be available to the Allround brand group, because R&D would be busy with other projects. They simply would not have the time to work on these projects outside of this schedule.

- Two slight reformulations of the Allround brand will be available from R&D for introduction in years two and three. Only one, if any, of these reformulations can be put into production, and the brand management team will have to decide at that time which of the available options to accept. R&D will provide the specifics of the potential reformulations at the end of year one. After year three the possibility of reformulation will be unavailable to the Allround brand group.

- Three potential line extensions will be available for commercial launch in years four and five. The team will have to choose among these three formulations for the line extension or choose not to introduce a brand extension at all. R&D will provide the specifics of these potential line extensions at the end of year three. After year five the potential line extensions will no longer be available from R&D.

- In years six and seven, three new product formulations will be available, including one based upon a product that is now available by prescription only. The Food and Drug Administration had indicated that these ingredients would be available for OTC cold and allergy product use at that time. R&D will provide the specifics of the potential products at the end of year five. Again R&D has a limited time frame for working on these new products. After year seven, the possibility of a new product line will be unavailable to the Allround brand group.

- In years eight and beyond, R&D will be able to reformulate Allround to the specifications provided by the brand management team.

Financial Situation

Allround is a successful and profitable brand with sales of $355.3 million at the manufacturer's level last year. The gross margin was $172.3 million, and the margin after advertising and promotional expenses was $145.3 million. The margin after all marketing expenditures including sales force and administrative costs was $129.5 million. The Allround brand also has to carry its share of fixed costs including the plant where Allround is produced and a share of corporate overhead charges. These charges were $62.4 million, leaving a net contribution of $67.2 million. The senior management of Allstar Brands expects the OCM group of the company to make even greater contributions in the future. The detailed income statement is presented in Exhibit 1.10.

The marketing budget received from the division will have to cover all sales force, advertising, and promotional expenditures as well as the cost to buy marketing research. The group was relieved to find that their budget had not been cut, and in fact is likely to be increased in the following year. These additional funds will allow them to purchase any marketing research that they deem necessary, as well as increase spending in one or more areas of their marketing mix.

Exhibit 1.10: OCM Group Income Statement

Manufacturer Sales	355.3		100.0%
Promotional Allowance	60.4		17.0%
Cost of Goods Sold	122.6		34.5%
Gross Margin		172.3	48.5%
Consumer & Trade Promo	7.0		2.0%
Advertising	20.0		5.6%
Sales Force	6.0		1.7%
Administrative	9.8		2.7%
Total Marketing Exp		42.8	12.0%
Contr after Marketing		129.5	36.5%
Fixed Costs		62.4	17.6%
Net Contribution		67.2	18.9%

The Marketing Task

The task of the Allround brand management team is to maintain long-term profitability and market share in the context of an increasingly competitive and changing environment. With great enthusiasm the OCM group sets out to do the job, each member with separate assignments, but all concerned with the performance of the Allround brand and any new brands that might be forthcoming. The team knows that it will be necessary to assess Allround's situation using the information presented in the exhibits and possibly other marketing research studies. After completing their analysis of the situation, the group will then make decisions in the areas of product choice, distribution, promotion, and pricing. They must keep in mind that all these decisions are interrelated and must be considered in context. The team will repeat this process over the coming ten years as they attempt to establish AllStar Brands as the leader in both profitability and market share in OTC cold medication.

Section 2: PharmaSim Operations Guide

PharmaSim has several different configurations and options available to the user:

- Multiple Scenarios with varying degrees of difficulty. The values in the exhibits correspond to scenarios 1-3, but not to others. There is also the possibility that you are using a customized scenario in which case the scenario choice screen will not appear. This may be the case if PharmaSim is being used as part of a educational program.

- Three playing levels with varying degrees of complexity. Level 1, or "Brand Assistant", has the fewest decisions and least number of reports available. Level 2, or "Assistant Brand Manager", is moderately complex. Level 3, or "Brand Manager", is the most complex and offers the greatest detail in decisions. Unless you specify otherwise, the default is to play at level 1 for two periods, then switch to level 2 for three periods, and finally, run the rest of the simulation at level 3. See the "Decisions" section of the manual for a further detail of the complexity of decisions made at each level.

More information about these options and configurations will be provided throughout the operations guide.

The remainder of this operations guide is divided into the following areas of coverage:

- Hardware Requirements and Installation

- Starting the Simulation / Choice of Scenarios

- Getting Around / Selecting Options (including graphing and sorting)

- Menu Overview

- Detail of Menu Options

- Reformulations and New Product Introductions

Hardware Requirements and Installation

In order to use the Windows compatible version of PharmaSim, your computer must already be set up to run Windows in either standard or enhanced mode, and you will need at least 4 megabytes of free RAM. Check your Microsoft Windows manual for minimum hardware requirements for Win95 or Windows 3.1. We recommend running off a hard drive for Windows users and backing up to the floppy disk. The minimum requirements are:

- An IBM-PC or compatible with Windows 3.1 or Win95 installed and running
- 4 megabytes of free RAM after Windows is loaded
- A 3 1/2" 1.44MB disk drive or network access
- 2 MB of hard disk space
- VGA graphics monitor

Note: Version 2.17 of PharmaSim is available for Apple Macintosh and MS-DOS systems.

Installation

To install PharmaSim for Windows 3.1, insert the player disk into drive A: (or whichever drive is the 3 1/2" drive). From the Windows File menu, Run A:\INSTALL. This will copy the program from the floppy to the hard drive, creating a PharmaSim directory (default directory is C:\Pharmasi). An ISI PharmaSim icon will be created in a Simulations group. Win95 is similar, but choose Run from the Start icon instead.

Note: If you are running PharmaSim over a network, your simulation administrator will provide instructions for using the software.

Starting the Simulation and Choice of Scenario and Level of Complexity

Once the installation process is complete, double click on the PharmaSim icon in the simulations group window. This will launch the program. After several seconds, you will be asked to register the product software. The registration information is especially important if you are using PharmaSim as part of a classroom exercise. Please follow any special instructions from your instructor. A sample registration screen is shown below.

The next screen will ask for the scenario and level of complexity. Again, if PharmaSim is part of a class, check with your professor as to which of these to select. The default progression and scenario 1 are recommended for first time users. A sample screen is shown below.

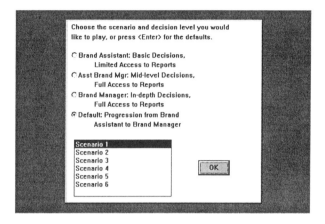

Notes: • In some situation, a custom scenario will be pre-loaded and no choice will be made.

• If you are playing the **competitive** version of the simulation against other members of your class or over the internet, you will not have the choice of scenario and level of complexity, nor will you be asked for registration information. Instead, you will be asked for the industry and firm name.

After selecting <OK>, the following screen will appear. This is the "about" screen. The <Getting Started> button will provide a brief overview of PharmaSim.

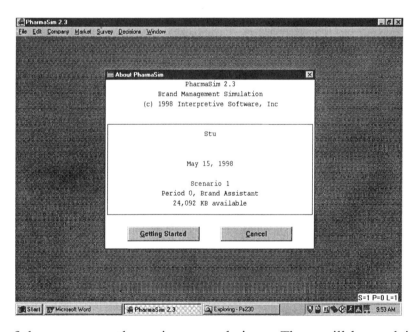

Across the top of the screen are the main menu choices. These will be explained later in this section.

Getting Around / Selecting Options

Control Buttons

A control button on a report or decision form allows you to choose an action to perform. Normally control buttons are found at the bottom or right hand side of screens. Just click on the button with your mouse to select it. You may also [Tab] to the button and press [Enter] or use the Ctrl key in combination with the highlighted letter (e.g. Ctrl-C = Cancel).

Sample control buttons: [Report] [Detail] [Next] [Segment] [Print] [Close]

List Boxes

A list box contains a list of choices. In most cases, you may select more than one of the choices. Click on the scroll bar to view all your choices, and select by clicking the mouse on the items to include.

Check Boxes and Radio Buttons

Check boxes and radio buttons allow you to select an option (usually yes or no, true or false). If you have a mouse, just click on the check box or radio button.

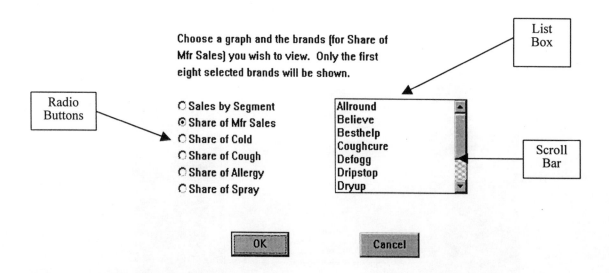

Graphing

Most reports may be graphed in order to gain a historical perspective and to identify important trends. On most reports, when you first select <Graph>, you'll be asked to either select a pre-defined graph from one of the radio buttons on the left side of the window, or select individual brands from a list box on the right side of the window. A sample graph of net income from the operating statistics report is shown below.

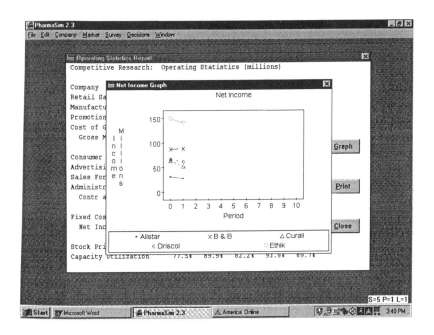

On line graphs displaying brand data, only 8 items may be viewed at once. These may be selected individually, or the default items chosen are the first eight items in the list box. For brand comparison graphs, the list box is sorted based on the sort criterion selected. Therefore, if the brands are currently sorted by market share, the default graph will be the top 8 brands in terms of market share.

To print a graph, select the PRINT menu option under the FILE menu.

Sorting

An additional analytical option on all the reports that compare brands is the <Sort> function. This will list the brands in the report in a selected, adding an additional dimension to the analysis. The sort options are listed below:

• by Name	Alphabetical / firm order. Helpful to see line extensions, firm product mix.
• by Category (Cold, Cough, Allergy, Nasal)	Highlights category competitors.
• by Manufacturer Sales	Shows the relationship of sales and a particular marketing factor. For instance, shelf space and sales. [Sort by sales from the shelf space report]
• by Price	Displays the relationship of price and a particular outcome. For example, price and purchase intentions. [Sort by price from purchase intentions report]
• by Advertising Expenditures	Same as above except using advertising expenditures.
• by Promotional Expenditures	Same as above except using promotion (co-op advertising, coupons, point of purchase, and trial size).

Using these sorting options can be a powerful tool for analysis as well as a helpful organizational aid. For instance, by sorting on advertising expenditures from the market share report, one can get a sense of the impact of advertising on market share. Graphing data also becomes easier as the graph list box will be ordered using the sort order. Since the default graph selections for most reports are the first eight brands in the list box, the sort order will determine which brands are graphed. Note that if particular brands are selected, these will be graphed and the sort order will have no impact on the brands displayed in the graph.

Menu Overview

To select a menu option, just use the mouse as you would with any Windows program. The main menu choices are always listed across the top of the PharmaSim window. You may access the menu at any time except when running the simulation. The entire menu structure for the individual version of the software is displayed in Exhibit 2.1.

As you can see in the exhibit, each of the main menu choices has a set of associated secondary menu options. The main menu topics are as follows:

File	• The FILE menu basically covers running the simulation (or replaying previous periods), changing your simulation complexity level, backing up files, printing options, and quitting the program.
Edit	• EDIT allows you to copy and paste items to and from the clipboard in Windows and Macintosh.
Company	• Menu items under COMPANY represent internal company reports that are prepared for the brand management team each year. These contain a number of good internal performance measurements. There is no charge for any of these reports. However, they contain no competitor or market intelligence information.
Market	• The MARKET menu contains all of the journal reports (free), competitive marketing intelligence reports ($), and reports on channels of distribution ($).
Survey	• Menu items under SURVEY are all part of the PharmaSim Consumer Survey ($). Once the database is purchased, all consumer survey reports are available.
Decisions	• The menu choices under DECISIONS are where the marketing plan and product decisions are entered. These menus will change with the levels and the current period (see below for more on levels). Once your firm has more than one brand in the market, it is necessary to select the brand at the bottom of the DECISIONS menu before entering your product plan.
Window	• The WINDOW menu contains general display and window options as well as help access.

Those menu options with a "$" next to them must be purchased and their cost comes out of the current period marketing budget. To find out the cost of this marketing research, see the INDUSTRY OUTLOOK option under MARKET.

Menu options that have are grayed out may not be available for the current playing level of the simulation, or for the customized version of the software you are using. Be sure to note when these are available as it indicates a special decision is to be made.

Exhibit 2.1 - PharmaSim Menu Structure (page # listed next to menu choice)

File	Edit	Company	Market	Survey	Decisions	Window

Advance to Next Period	p. 25
Replay Period	p. 25
Restart Simulation	p. 26
Change Simulation Level	p. 26
Backup Files	p. 26
Printer Setup	p. 26
Print	p. 26
Print Reports	p. 26
Administrator Report	p. 27
Quit	p. 27

Income Statement	p. 28
Product Contribution	p. 29
Sales Report	p. 30
Promotion Report	p. 31
Portfolio Graph	p. 32

Marketing Update	p. 33
Industry Outlook	p. 34
Symptoms Reported	p. 35
Brand Formulations	p. 36
Share of Mfr Sales	p. 37
Operating Statistics $	p. 38
Sales Force $	p. 39
Advertising $	p. 40
Promotion $	p. 41
Share of Channel Sales $	p. 42
Pricing $	p. 43
Shopping Habits $	p. 45
Shelf Space $	p. 46
Recommendations $	p. 47

Purchase Survey $	p. 48
Segmentation	p. 48
Brands Purchased	p. 49
Purchase Intentions	p. 51
Satisfaction	p. 52
Brand Awareness	p. 53
Decision Criteria	p. 54
Brand Perception	p. 55
Tradeoffs	p. 56

Add or Change Product	p. 66
Discontinue Product	p. 66
Sales Force	p. 57
Product Input	p. 57
Budget Allocation	p. 58
What if...	p. 59
Allround	

Switch to Window
Close All Windows
Font
Help
About

Menu Detail

Each menu option is described on the following pages along with a sample screen display where appropriate. The order of the descriptions corresponds to the order of the main menu and its options.

The general process for going through the menus is to review the information in the COMPANY, MARKET, and SURVEY menus, then make decisions using the DECISIONS menu, and finally advance the simulation using the FILE - ADVANCE TO NEXT PERIOD option. All decisions are saved automatically as you make them. Our only suggestions are to periodically make a secondary copy of the database using the BACKUP FILES option, and to print out an administrator's report after the simulation is advanced.

File - Advance to Next Period

After all decisions have been entered and checked, it is time to advance the simulation to the next period. Be sure that you are completely satisfied with your decisions and that you are within the budget limit before using this menu option. If you fail to review any of the decision screens or are over budget, you will be notified when you attempt to advance the simulation.

Sales Force + Adv + Consumer & Trade Promo + Research <= BUDGET

Advancing the simulation to the next period moves the calendar ahead one year, generating an updated set of reports for the new year. As the simulation runs, a "PharmaSim Marketing Update" is created, highlighting some of the major events of the simulated year. These include product introductions, overall levels of advertising, promotional spending, and total market sales. The marketing update report is available under MARKET - MARKETING UPDATE every period.

Once the marketing update is completed, the simulation has been advanced. All the reports now reflect what has just occurred in the simulated year. The lower right corner of your screen will display the new period. In addition, if you are using the default level, your level may have changed as well.

Before doing anything else, we'd suggest that you print an Administrator's Report using FILE - ADMINISTRATOR REPORT. This will give you a hard copy of your decisions and a summary of your results. Save this printout as a record of your performance and as a "just in case" copy of your decisions should your simulation database get corrupted. If you are running off a hard drive, it is a good idea to make a back up copy of your database using the FILE - BACKUP FILES option. The back-up copy may be either on a blank floppy disk or on the original PharmaSim disk. Again, this is a precautionary measure that only takes a few moments and is well worth it should you have a disk failure.

File - Replay Period

This allows you to return to the previous period. Think of it as an "undo" for running the simulation. This can be very important if you made an error in entering your decisions or if you want to experiment using different decisions. If you are in a classroom situation, you may be asked to inform your instructor why it was necessary to rerun a period. Also, if you are using a customized version of PharmaSim, this option may be grayed out and unavailable.

File - Restart Simulation

This option erases the current game and resets all data to period 0. A warning message will appear indicating that you will destroy simulation data before the game is restarted. Therefore, you must be certain that it is your intent to destroy all of your simulation before selecting this option. This is, in effect, starting over; and there is no undo.

File - Change Simulation Level

This allows you to change the current level of play. The default level plays two periods at level 1 ("Brand Assistant"), three periods at level 2 ("Assistant Brand Manager"), and the rest at level 3 ("Brand Manager"). The levels are described in greater detail under the DECISION menu.

File - Backup Files

Use this option to make a copy of the database files, typically on a floppy disk. We recommend backing up the database after each simulation run as insurance. If you backup to your original program disk you may reinstall the simulation and pick up where you left off. In addition, the simulation administrator may use this backup disk may be used for summary presentations.

File - Printer Setup

Choosing this option brings up the standard printer dialog box in Windows. Should you need to change printers, please do so through the operating system. For instance, use the printer settings under the Start menu in Windows 95.

File - Print

Choosing PRINT from the FILE menu will print out the currently active window (report or graph). On reports, this is the same as selecting the <PRINT> button at the bottom of the window. For graphs, this is the only way to print.

File - Print Reports

The PRINT REPORTS menu choice allows printing of multiple reports rather than printing each report separately using the <PRINT> button. However, if time is limited it may make sense to print out the reports in a batch mode using the PRINT REPORTS option.

There are four basic groups of reports you can print from this menu.

1. Company Reports
2. Market Reports (some free, some $)
3. Survey Reports (uses current segmentation approach)
4. Current Decisions (when you have completed input)

The reports correspond to the COMPANY, MARKET, SURVEY, and DECISIONS main menu choices. Thus, if you select COMPANY, all of the reports under the COMPANY menu option (Income Statement, Product Contribution, Sales Report, and the Promotion Report) will print.

Likewise, if you select MARKET, all of the market, competitive, and distribution reports will print.

There are three issues to note. First, if a particular study has not been purchased (such as operating statistics), that study will not be printed. Second, in level 1 only studies available for level 1 will print. Third, when printing the survey reports, the current segmentation scheme will be used. Thus, if the last segmentation selected in the market survey was cold and young families, all the survey reports will print using that segmentation scheme. In general, the print options will print all free and purchased reports available at your current level of play.

File - Print Administrator Report

The ADMINISTRATOR REPORT generates a summary of decisions and results for the current period. The administrator report is typically turned into the simulation administrator at the end of each period. It is probably worthwhile to print an extra copy for your own records because it is a good summary of key decisions and results. In addition, if you need to reconstruct your current situation because of a computer malfunction or loss of diskette, you will need these reports for accuracy. Previous administrator reports may be printed at any time by typing in the appropriate period.

File - Quit

Selecting QUIT will exit the PharmaSim program. All of your current decisions and results are automatically saved. When you run PharmaSim again, you will be where you left off. If you are running off of the floppy disk, please leave the disk in the drive when you exit the program until the program is finished with the exit routine and returns you to the operating system.

Edit - Copy

Select this menu option to copy the contents of the current screen into the clipboard on Windows and Macintosh machines. The contents may then be pasted into other applications programs such as word processors, spreadsheets, or graphics programs.

Company - Income Statement

The income statement shows the overall results for Allstar Brands with a breakdown by major expenditures. Each item is also displayed as a percent of manufacturer sales (not retail) for comparative purposes.

Base Cost*:   No Charge
Available*:   All levels
Sort*:   N/A
Graphs*:   Manufacturers Sales, Promotional Allowance, Sales Force Expense,
                Advertising Expense, Promotion Expense, Net Income

```
Firm Income Report                                              [X]
Company Results: Income Statement          Firm: Allstar

Manufacturer Sales      355.3               100.0%
Promotional Allowance    60.4                17.0%
Cost of Goods Sold      122.6                34.5%
   Gross Margin                   172.3      48.5%
                                                     ┌──────────┐
Consumer & Trade Promo    7.0                 2.0%   │  Graph   │
Advertising              20.0                 5.6%   └──────────┘
Sales Force               6.0                 1.7%
Administrative            9.8                 2.7%   ┌──────────┐
   Total Marketing Exp            42.8       12.0%   │  Print   │
                                                     └──────────┘
Contr after Mktg                 129.5       36.5%
                                                     ┌──────────┐
Fixed Costs                       62.4       17.6%   │  Close   │
                                                     └──────────┘
Net Income                        67.2       18.9%
Next Period Budget                34.2        9.6%

Note: Figures are in millions of dollars
```

Manufacturer sales are receipts from all direct sales to distributors and wholesalers net of volume discounts. The promotional allowance is based on the promotional allowance percentage for each channel (10-20%) and sales to that channel. The cost of goods sold is the total variable manufacturing cost of all brands combined. The gross margin is manufacturer sales less the promotional allowance and cost of goods sold.

Promotion, advertising, and sales force are based on your firm's decisions and comprise budget expenditures. Administrative expenses include some fixed overhead, some variable expenses, and some expenses related to the number of orders placed. Additionally, all market research costs are included in this expense category. These are then combined to generate total marketing expenditures that are then subtracted from the gross margin to calculate contribution after marketing. The fixed costs (plants and overhead) are then subtracted to arrive at the net income. A significant portion of net income for the OTC division is applied to other corporate costs such as R&D, typically an expensive item in pharmaceutical companies.

Each company's plants can accommodate several product lines due to flexible manufacturing techniques. However, *once capacity is built it cannot be decreased*. Plant capacity expands in 20 million unit increments automatically when demand exceeds current capacity. Forecasting product demand is especially important in this context, as fixed cost per unit is significantly lower at 99% versus 80% of capacity. There are also economies of scale to consider. As production and capacity increase, per unit costs decrease assuming the same capacity utilization.

Next period budget is calculated using your firm's current budget expenditures, performance, and product requirements. This budget must cover the coming period's expenditures on promotion (not including the allowance), advertising, sales force, and marketing research reports.

Company - Product Contribution

The product contribution statement shows a similar breakdown as the income statement, but on a product level instead. Only costs that are directly linked to a particular product are displayed. Since this is an internal accounting report, only Allstar's products are displayed. Selecting <Next> will display other products once they have been introduced.

Base Cost*:   No Charge
Available*:   All levels
Sort*:   N/A
Graphs*:   Product Contribution for all brands

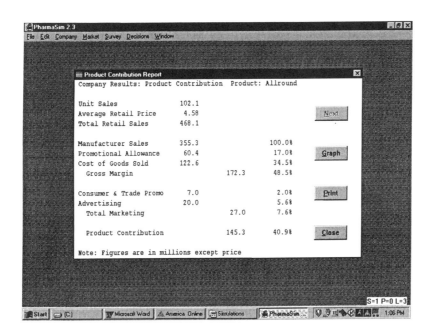

Unit sales represent the total amount of units purchased at retail stores across the country. The average retail price is the average price paid for this brand by the consumer. These two values multiplied together equal total retail sales in dollars. Manufacturer sales include all direct sales to the channel and sales to wholesalers. Therefore, the difference between retail sales and manufacturer sales is the markup taken by retailers and wholesalers. The cost of goods sold is based on the number of active ingredients in the brand, as well as the form (tablet, liquid, or spray). Advertising, consumer and trade promotions are directly from the decisions.

---

* The base cost represents the cost of ordering the report at the beginning of the simulation. This cost will be adjusted by inflation as the game progresses. Some reports or decisions are not available at level 1 or 2. Graph, sort, and detail options available as noted.

Company - Sales Report

The Sales Report summarizes the unit and dollar sales volume generated through direct and indirect distribution for each product. The direct sales are grouped initially by volume discount, and secondly by retail sales outlet. This report will provide important feedback on discount schedules and price to wholesaler, as well as direct and wholesaler sales force effectiveness. Selecting <Next> will display other products once they have been introduced.

Base Cost:	No Charge
Available:	Levels 2 & 3
Sort:	N/A
Graphs:	Product Sales

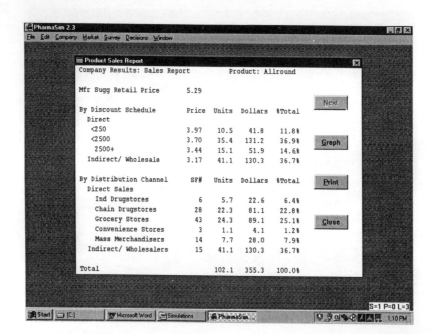

The sales breakdown by discount schedule reflects not only the effect of different price/volume discounts, but also the type of retail outlet is being served. For instance, if the majority of direct sales are to independent drugstores (typically smaller accounts), it is likely that more sales will be at lower volumes. Likewise, if your firm is generating a majority of sales through mass merchandisers (typically larger accounts), it is likely that larger volume discounts will be used.

The sales breakdown by distribution channel provides information on sales to distributors. Note that the sales through the wholesaler ultimately are sold in the five retail outlets. Therefore, be cautious about using this report as an indication of retail sales of product and instead use the SHARE OF CHANNEL SALES report. Sales force allocation by distribution channel is also provided in this report to help compare sales force allocation with sales by channel.

Company - Promotion Report

The Promotion Report summarizes a firm's promotional results for the period. There are five different types of consumer and trade promotion. In this report, you will receive feedback from the market as to the success of your promotional plan. Each aspect of the promotional plan is described below. Selecting <Next> will display other products once they have been introduced.

Base Cost: No Charge
Available: Levels 2 & 3
Sort: N/A
Graphs: Trade Rating

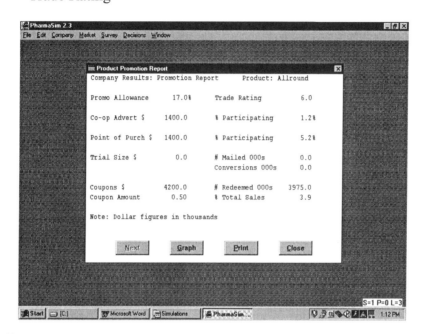

Promotional Allowances: Average promotional allowance for the five retail outlets and the wholesaler. Promotional allowances are a non-budget item.

Trade Rating: The rating is a summarized result from a survey of retailers and wholesalers on trade support and practices offered by your company. The trade rating value is scaled from 1 to 10, where 10 is the high value. This value is on a product basis and may be graphed.

Co-op Advertising: Budget available to retailers for jointly advertising a product. The cost of the advertisement is divided between the manufacturer and the retailer. The % participation rate represents the percent of retailers who used a co-op advertising allowance with this brand.

Point-of-Purchase: Total budget allotted to creating, producing, distributing, and maintaining point-of-purchase displays in retail outlets. The % participation rate represents the percent of retailers who used a point-of-purchase display for this product at some point during the year.

Trial Size: Total budget spent on producing and distributing free trial size samples to households. The number mailed and conversion values represent the total number of trial samples mailed and an estimate of how many of these households then converted to this brand.

Coupons: Budget allocated to printing, distributing, and redeeming consumer coupons. The total number of redemptions and the percent of total unit sales attributed to coupons are also reported.

Company - Portfolio Graph

The Portfolio Graph menu option displays your current product portfolio in a 2 x 2 growth-share matrix. See section 4 for a more thorough discussion of resource allocation and product portfolio issues.

Base Cost: No Charge
Available: Level 3
Sort: N/A
Graphs: As shown below

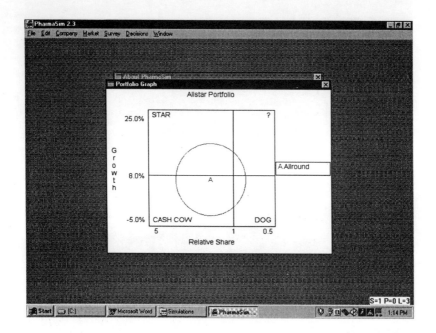

Market Definition: Each Strategic Business Unit (SBU) corresponds to a brand or line extension. The market is defined as cold, cough, allergy, or nasal spray as shown in the SHARE OF MFR SALES under MARKET.

Growth: The market growth of the segment where the brand competes determines the position of the SBU on the vertical axis. Thus, for Allround in period 0, the cold market grew at 6.6% and therefore Allround is placed just under the 8% market growth line.

Relative Share: A brand's strength in the marketplace is often measured by its relative market share. This is calculated by taking the brand's market share and dividing it by the market share of its largest competitor. In period 0 for Allround, its share of the cold medicine market is 40.4%, while Besthelp, its largest competitor, has 25.2% share. Therefore, Allround's relative market share is 40.4 / 25.2 = 1.6, placing Allround to the left of the vertical line representing a relative share of 1. This indicates that Allround is a "cash cow" and should be a good source of funds for marketing expenditures and new brand introductions.

Market - Marketing Update

Advancing the simulation creates a "PharmaSim Marketing Update" screen highlighting some of the major events of the year, such as product introductions, overall levels of advertising and promotional spending, and total market sales. This menu option re-displays that screen.

Base Cost: No Charge
Available: All levels
Sort: N/A
Graphs: None

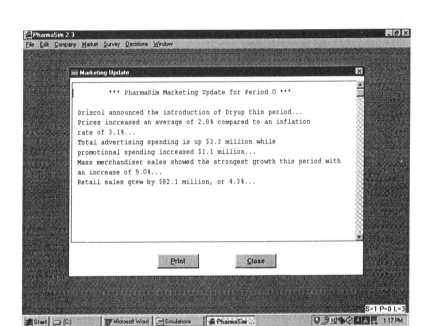

If you are able to reformulate a product or introduce a line extension or new product, this will be displayed as well.

If you change levels (e.g. from Brand Assistant to Assistant Brand Manager), this will be noted at the bottom of the listing. Select < Getting Started > from the WINDOW - ABOUT menu for more information about how the change in levels affects your responsibilities.

Market - Industry Outlook

The Industry Outlook is a trade publication that reports general economic and industry conditions, cost of sales force, and cost of market research. All of the values represent costs or estimates for the coming year.

Base Cost: No Charge
Available: All levels
Sort: N/A
Graphs: None

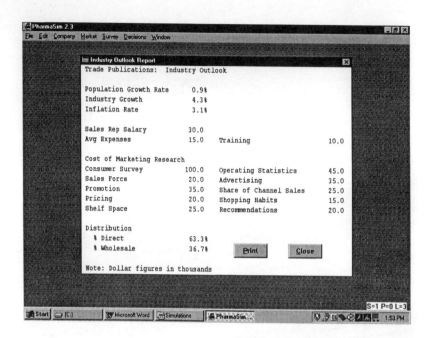

The general economic variables of population growth, industry growth, and inflation are estimates for the coming year. These variables may provide a basis for overall demand and price/cost forecasts. The report also displays the cost of a salesperson's salary and expenses, as well as training costs for new hires. Typically, sales force turnover runs 10-20% each year. Therefore, even maintaining current sales force levels will incur a significant training cost. In the above example, each experienced salesperson will cost $45,000, and each new hire will cost $55,000.

The estimated cost for each of the competitive and market research reports is also reported. Each of these reports offers insight into the competitive dynamics of other firms and feedback from distribution channels. The charge for each report is assessed on-line when the study is ordered and will be subtracted from the current period budget.

At the bottom of this screen is an estimate of the percentage of sales which is distributed directly and through wholesalers to retailers. These values represent total industry sales of all five firms. As is the case in all of the market research studies, some error is to be expected. Often, these values are the result of surveys or sampled information that is subject to some distortion.

Market - Symptoms Reported

The Symptoms Reported publication gives an overview of the basic cold related symptoms reported over the past year. The percentage shown is for the entire PharmaSim population. This estimate is published yearly and is widely available in trade journals.

Base Cost:	No Charge
Available:	All levels
Sort:	N/A
Graphs:	None

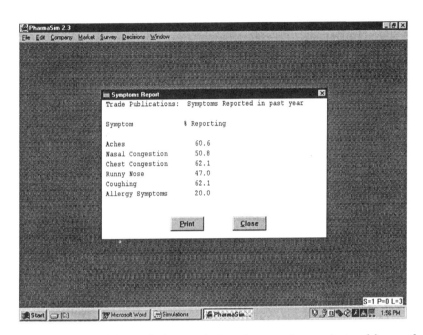

This report provides a rough idea of demand for the products that address these symptoms. However, this report does not take into account medication usage that may affect demand considerably. For instance, fewer people suffer from allergy symptoms than from nasal congestion, but usage of allergy medication per person is considerably higher than for cold medicine in general.

Each brand on the market attempts to relieve some or all of these symptoms. As discussed in greater depth later, the brand formulation report provides a listing of the ingredients in each brand, and the market survey of brand perceptions shows how consumers perceive the effectiveness of each brand against these symptoms.

Market - Brand Formulations

The Brand Formulations publication displays the current amount of active ingredients in each brand on the market as well as the current FDA maximum allowable limit for each ingredient (based on 4 doses in a 24 hour period). This report will highlight any new changes in form or content.

Base Cost:	No Charge
Available:	All levels
Sort:	Yes
Graphs:	None

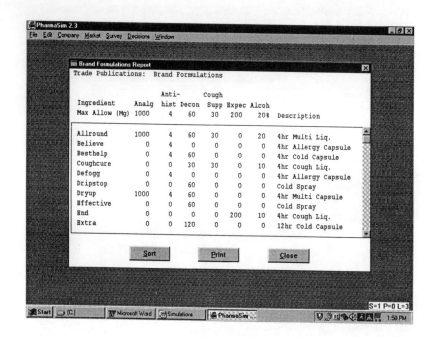

The first letter of each brand signifies the company that manufactures the product. For instance, Driscol manufactures all brands starting with D. Brand line extensions are denoted with a "+" following the name. For example, if an Extra+ were on the market, it would be a line extension to the Extra brand name. Typically, these line extensions offer similar benefits to the original brand. Each brand has one or more active ingredients that cannot exceed the maximum allowable dosage in a four-hour period (or four doses in a 24-hour period). 12-hour formulations are allowed to have twice the maximum, since the dosage frequency is twice per day. The packaging for the 12-hour capsules contains half as many capsules as the 4-hour (so that pricing is for equivalent per 24 hours of relief). Each of the active ingredients are described below:

Analgesics:	Reduce fevers and relieves head and body aches.
Antihistamines:	Relieve itchy eyes and sneezing.
Decongestant:	Reduces nasal congestion by shrinking swollen nasal passages.
Cough Suppressant:	Suppresses coughing reflex.
Expectorant:	Loosens chest congestion to improve the effectiveness of coughing.
Alcohol:	Helps people rest and numbs the pain.

Market - Share of Manufacturer Sales

The Share of Manufacturer Sales publication contains estimates of each brand's market share by product category. Under this report, each brand can only be in one category. Therefore, multi-symptom brands such as Allround are listed in the cold category even though they may be used for cough or allergy symptoms from time to time. For purposes of this report, if the brand is labeled for a particular use it is placed under that category.

Base Cost:	No Charge
Available:	All levels
Sort:	Yes
Graphs:	Sales by Segment
	Share of Manufacturer Sales
	Share by Product Category (4)

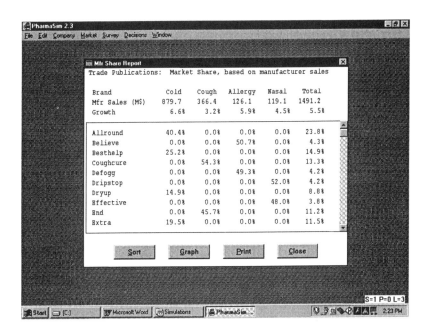

This report provides an estimate of total manufacturer sales in each product/market category. Product market shares listed in this report will differ from the values estimated from retail sales because of different sources of data and different price/discount schedules among brands. Retail sales are estimated based on end user prices, whereas manufacturer sales are based solely on sales to distribution channels. The market shares calculated in the market survey of brands purchased will also be different because the values are based on unit sales and exclude price differences. Therefore, in PharmaSim there are three different measures of market share -- share of manufacturer sales ($), share of retail sales ($), and share of consumer purchases (units).

Market - Operating Statistics

The competitive research on operating statistics shows an estimated contribution statement for each of the five firms. This information may be used to analyze differences in resource allocation and costs.

Base Cost: $45,000
Available: All levels
Sort: N/A
Graphs: Share of Manufacturer Sales
                  Manufacturer Sales by Firm
                  Promotion Allowance Expenditures
                  Consumer and Trade Promotion
                  Advertising Expenditures
                  Sales Force Expenditures
                  Net Income
                  Stock Price
                  Capacity Utilization

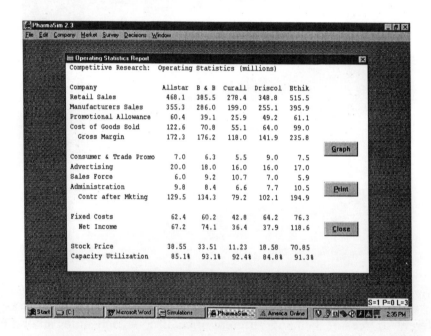

Company	Allstar	B & B	Curall	Driscol	Ethik
Retail Sales	468.1	385.5	278.4	348.8	515.5
Manufacturers Sales	355.3	286.0	199.0	255.1	395.9
Promotional Allowance	60.4	39.1	25.9	49.2	61.1
Cost of Goods Sold	122.6	70.8	55.1	64.0	99.0
Gross Margin	172.3	176.2	118.0	141.9	235.8
Consumer & Trade Promo	7.0	6.3	5.5	9.0	7.5
Advertising	20.0	18.0	16.0	16.0	17.0
Sales Force	6.0	9.2	10.7	7.0	5.9
Administration	9.8	8.4	6.6	7.7	10.5
Contr after Mkting	129.5	134.3	79.2	102.1	194.9
Fixed Costs	62.4	60.2	42.8	64.2	76.3
Net Income	67.2	74.1	36.4	37.9	118.6
Stock Price	38.55	33.51	11.23	18.58	70.85
Capacity Utilization	85.1%	93.1%	92.4%	84.8%	91.3%

This report provides similar information as your firm's income statement, except now for your competitors. There are three differences, however. First, there is no value for your competitor's budget. One possibility for estimating this value is to base it on last year's budget expenditures for each competitive firm. This would involve adding the spending for advertising, promotion, and sales force. The second difference from the firm income statement is the addition of an industry consultant's estimate of capacity utilization. This could have strategic implications for your firm. For instance, if your competitors are significantly under full capacity, you might expect them to try to gain share through aggressive pricing or heavy marketing expenditures. The third difference is the addition of a stock price. This can be used as one possible measurement of your performance over time.

Market - Sales Force

The competitive research on sales force estimates displays how each firm has decided to allocate its sales personnel. Sales force personnel includes both direct sales and indirect/support functions. This report provides information as to which channels the competition is targeting, and what levels of channel/wholesaler support might be necessary in order to be competitive.

Base Cost:	$20,000
Available:	Levels 2 & 3
Sort:	N/A
Graphs:	Total Sales Force
	Sales Force by Channel (5)

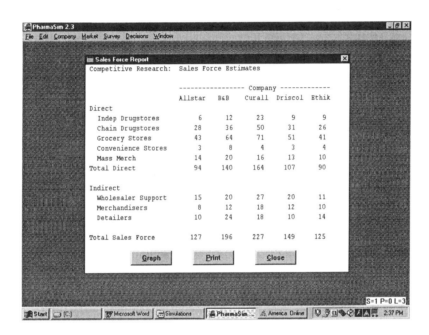

The direct sales force includes sales reps and in-house sales personnel who support the retail channels. The direct sales force take orders and provide administrative assistance, while the field sales force aid the channel with services such as stocking and pricing products. Both groups distribute large amounts of product literature and educate the channels with industry and company information. In addition, they often attend regional trade and association meetings.

The wholesaler support sales force provides similar services, but tailored to the wholesale channel. Typically, fewer support personnel are needed for wholesalers because they are more concentrated and provide a number of services of their own. Merchandisers and detailers represent auxiliary sales personnel not directly involved in selling products. Merchandisers maintain point-of-purchase displays and manage retail shelf-space. Detailers work directly with doctors and pharmacists to generate product support and recommendations for a company's brands. Merchandising and detailing are especially important for successful new product introductions.

Market - Advertising

The competitive research on advertising estimates compares media expenditures, advertising agency, and the basic message for each brand. The analysis of the advertising message is derived from a compilation of each of the advertising campaigns for the brands.

Base Cost: $35,000
Available: Levels 2 & 3
Sort: Yes
Graphs: Advertising Expenditures by Brand

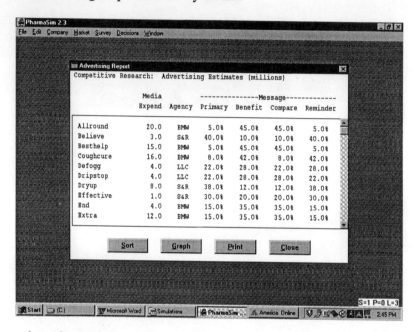

Media expenditure is estimated through a compilation of network and spot television charges and uses. This value is then verified through industry and company sources. The agency listed is the company that manages a particular brand's accounts. These agencies are described below:

Agency	Quality	Cost (% of media expend.)
Brewster, Maxwell and Wheeler (BMW)	High	15%
Sully & Rodgers (S&R)	Mid	10%
Lester Loebol & Company (LLC)	Low	5%

An industry media analyst compiles the message percentage in the report based on the content of each brand's commercials. The strategy behind each approach is described below:

Message: Primary   - Creates awareness and stimulates primary demand
            Benefits   - Emphasizes product benefits to consumer
            Comparison   - Compares product with competitor
            Reminder   - Maintains awareness and stimulates repurchase

---

*Note: In reality, an advertising agency would not work with competing companies because of conflict of interest. For simplicity, these three agencies have been used to represent the different options with regard to quality of message and cost.

Market - Promotion

The competitive research on promotional activity monitors the retail outlets and trade sources to estimate each brand's promotional expenditures on allowances, co-op advertising, and point-of-purchase displays. The report is unable to estimate expenditures on coupons or trials, but does indicate whether these approaches were used during the past year.

Base Cost: $35,000
Available: Levels 2 & 3
Sort: Yes
Graphs: Promotion Allowance
                  Promotion Expenditures ($)

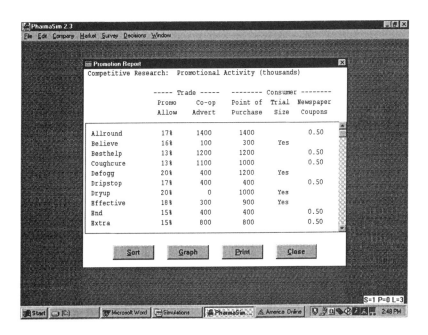

The promotion allowance is the average allowance for the five retail outlets and wholesalers for each brand. The minimum value that an outlet will accept is 10%, while the industry's accepted maximum promotion allowance is 20%. This allowance is given as a percent of the price to the channel and typically is used for the cost of stocking, price discounts, and brand promotion in the outlet. In many ways, this can be viewed as an additional discount to the channel. Co-op advertising displays the amount used for joint advertising between the manufacturer and retailer. The estimate is from retail channel sources. Point of purchase expenditures estimate the amount spent on creating, producing, distributing, and maintaining point of purchase displays in retail outlets. The trial size and coupons listings indicate whether these consumer promotion approaches were used during the past year, and for coupons, the face amount.

Market - Share of Channel Sales

The market research report on share of channel sales displays market share by retail distribution outlet. This report is based on retail sales, as opposed to unit sales or manufacturer sales. There is also an estimate of the total sales and sales growth rate for each retail category.

Base Cost: $25,000
Available: All levels except brand detail only at level 3
Sort: Yes
Graphs: Sales by Channel
                    Share of Retail Sales
                    Share of Retail Sales by Channel (5)
Brand List: Click on a brand to display unit sales by channel / discount

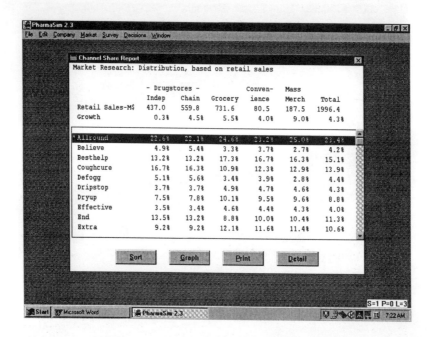

This report addresses three issues. First, it provides information about the volume and growth of sales through particular channels. These values are displayed at the top of the report. For instance, in the above screen, grocery stores have by far the largest amount of sales ($731.6 million) and a good growth rate (5.5%).

The second issue addressed in this report is each product's share of sales in each channel. Share by channel is likely to vary due to consumer shopping habits, pricing policies, and sales force distribution. To gain further insight into this data, your firm may want to look at the market research report on shopping habits and pricing, or the competitor report on sales force.

Finally, clicking on a brand will break down unit sales by price discount and channel (the same detail report available in the pricing report). Many of your decisions will influence your share and volume in a particular sales channel. Volume discounts, promotion, and sales force all affect how much support and shelf space your brand receives.

Market - Pricing

The market research report on average retail price displays each brand's manufacturer suggested retail price and actual selling price by channel. This report will give an indication of discount levels in the industry across brands and channels.

Base Cost: $20,000
Available: All levels except brand detail only at level 3
Sort: Yes
Graphs: MSRP by Brand
Brand List: Click on a brand to display brand unit sales by discount / channel

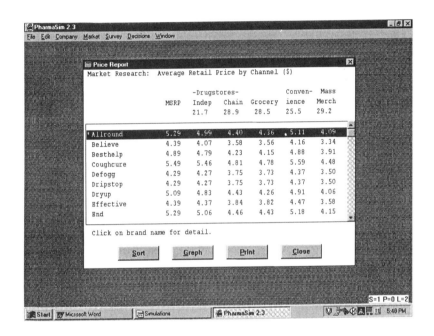

Competitive pricing is a key issue in PharmaSim. Comparing manufacturer suggested retail prices (MSRP) is a good indicator of where your brand is positioned on a price basis. However, it is important to also analyze 'the actual retail price on a channel basis since consumers ultimately pay this price for the product.

Each retail channel has a different pricing structure and uses different markups for different brands. Furthermore, most brands have different volume discounts and promotional allowances that will also affect actual retail prices.

Clicking on a brand breaks down unit sales by price discount and channel (the same detail report available in the share of channel sales report). Carefully analyze how each retailer uses the volume discounts. Remember that many of the retail stores use wholesalers, so your pricing structure to wholesalers is an additional factor to consider.

Market - Share of Channel Sales / Pricing - Detail

The detail of the both the Share of Channel Sales and Pricing reports provides in-depth information on sales by channel and level of pricing discount. Basically, rather than providing a "slice" of information across brands, this report provides more detailed information on channel sales by brand. This report is available for all products in the market.

Base Cost: Part of the Share of Channel Sales or Pricing Report
Available: Level 3 only
Sort: N/A
Graphs: None
Next: Displays the next brand listed in the pricing or share report

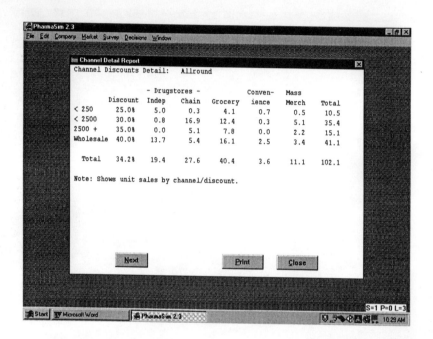

The detailed channel sales and price discount report provides information on how sales of each brand flow through direct and wholesale distribution. Sales by volume discount vary considerably depending on the distribution channel. Overall sales by distribution channel are also provided. This information may be of great assistance determining sales force allocation, pricing discounts, and promotional allowances.

Market - Shopping Habits

This market research report estimates shopping preferences for each type of illness. The report may be used to help determine sales force allocation and promotional strategy for each brand.

Base Cost:	$15,000
Available:	Levels 2 & 3
Sort:	N/A
Graphs:	Shopping Habits by Product Category

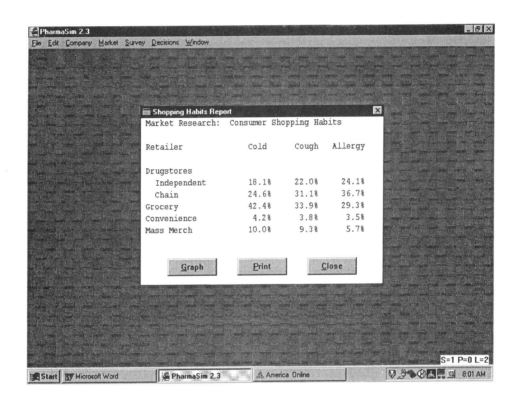

The channels where consumers shop for cold medications should be an important factor influencing your firm's strategy. For instance, a brand targeted for cold sufferers might choose to emphasize grocery stores more heavily than a brand for allergy sufferers. In the above example, over 42% of cold medication is purchased in grocery stores, whereas allergy medication is more likely to be purchased in drugstores.

Just like consumers, different channels have different needs. For example, mass merchandisers may prefer discounts to sales force support, whereas independent drugstores may appreciate the additional support services of salespeople and wholesalers.

In addition, be aware of how competitors use channel support. Sometimes opportunities arise in distribution because of neglect (or over-emphasis) of a particular channel by other companies.

Market - Shelf Space

The market research report on shelf space estimates how much space the retail channels allocate to each brand. This can be important feedback for promotional allowances and other trade and consumer promotion.

Base Cost: $25,000
Available: Levels 2 & 3
Sort: Yes
Graphs: Average Shelf Space (all channels)

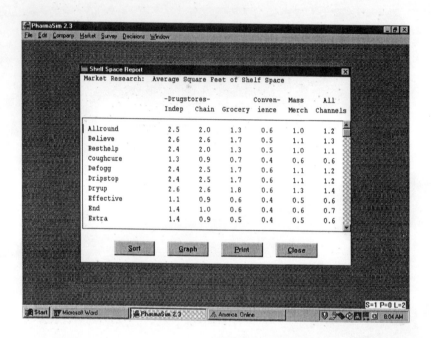

One of the key strategic ingredients for an OTC brand is gaining prime shelf space. This report displays the average amount of shelf space given to each brand. Retailers typically give more shelf space to the most profitable brands. The retail outlet will usually consider profit in terms of the margin earned per unit (including volume discounts and promotional allowances) and product turnover (the number of units sold in a year). However, some retailers also take advantage of co-op advertising to draw customers into their store. Sales force, especially merchandisers, also influences the amount of shelf space allocated to brands.

Market - Recommendations

The market research report on recommendations surveys several hundred physicians and pharmacists as to what brands they would recommend to patients reporting particular ailments. This report is especially useful for companies who target segments that are more inclined to request a recommendation from a doctor or pharmacist.

Base Cost:	$20,000
Available:	Levels 2 & 3
Sort:	Yes
Graphs:	Recommendations by Product Category and Brand

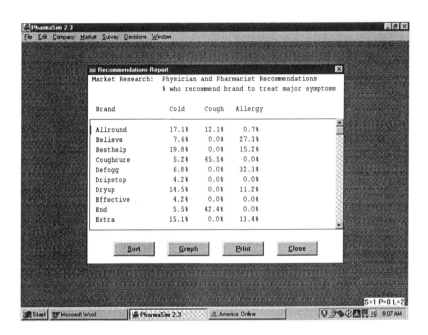

Often, when consumers are unsure which brand might best relieve certain symptoms they look to physicians and pharmacists for guidance. This report shows the results of a trade survey of family physicians and pharmacists. Each respondent was asked to rate which brand was most effective against a particular illness, taking into consideration side effects such as drowsiness, alcohol content, or unnecessary medication.

The recommendation report is a good indicator of the underlying medicinal value of a brand without the effect of advertising, promotion, or pricing on the consumer. Doctors and pharmacists typically have good knowledge about most brands on the market and are not especially influenced by consumer deals. Of course, like consumers, they may be more aware of some brands than others. Physicians may also be influenced by the manufacturer's detailer sales force, which provide free samples and product literature.

Market Survey - Description

The marketing survey is a tabulation of results from a series of questionnaires distributed by a marketing research company that serves the cold medicine market. Basically, the survey is a consumer database that may be analyzed through a number of different studies. To access any of these studies, the entire survey must be ordered. At the Brand Assistant level (level 1), segmentation is not available.

Base Cost: $100,000
Available: All levels
Sort: N/A
Graphs: See individual reports on the following pages.

The Market Survey provides seven reports:

1. Brands purchased by consumers
2. Comparison of purchase intentions and actual purchases
3. Customer satisfaction with brands
4. Brand awareness, trials, and repurchases
5. Criteria used in making purchase decision; penetration and usage
6. Consumer perception of product effectiveness for various symptoms (graph)
7. Perceived tradeoffs between price and effectiveness (graph)

Reports 1-3 are based on unit sales, which take into account usage rates (i.e. multiple purchases by a consumer are counted multiple times), whereas reports 4-7 are based on the purchasing population (i.e. multiple purchasers are only counted once).

The segmentation option provides market survey data segmented by any target group. The two segmentation schemes are illness and household/family demographics. This cross-section analysis may provide a better understanding of the consumer needs which are driving the market. The input screen for segmentation is shown below and can be accessed either through the SEGMENTATION menu option or through the <Xsection> control button on the individual reports.

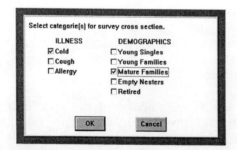

You may place an 'x' in more than one segment. Selecting two or more in the same column will view respondents who meet any one of those criteria. Marking in separate columns means the respondent must meet both criteria. For instance, marking Cold and Mature Families will provide results from only those respondents who meet both criteria. Marking Cold and Cough will display results from cold or cough sufferers from any demographic section (or, all non-allergy respondents). If no items are marked, then data based on all respondents are displayed. The top of the market survey reports will indicate the chosen cross-section. Once the database is purchased, there is no limit on the quantity of cross sections or reports in a given period.

Survey - Brands Purchased

The market survey of brands purchased estimates market share for each brand based on unit sales. This analysis can be segmented to view a brand's strengths or weaknesses across different consumer demographics. The survey differs from both the manufacturer market share and retail sales market share because it is based on units sold and product price has no impact.

Base Cost: Part of $100,000 Market Survey
Available: Cross Section -- Levels 2 & 3
                        Overall Only -- Level 1
Sort: Yes
Graphs: Cross Section of Market Share by Brand
Brand List: Click on a brand to display detailed purchase information.

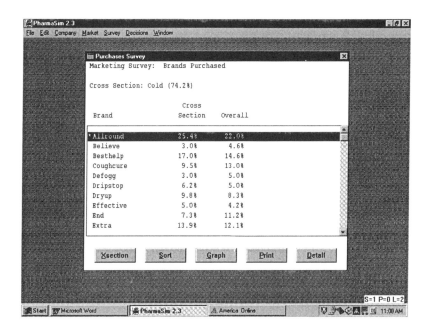

The above example shows that Allround and Besthelp have a higher market share of cold sufferers than overall. This is to be expected as few Allround users are seeking allergy relief and few Besthelp purchasers are using the medicine for coughs. Conversely, allergy and cough medicines show lower market share in this cross-section as to be expected. The report also indicates that cold sufferers represent 74.2% of all "cold" medicine purchases, much larger than either coughs or allergy purchasers.

Survey - Brands Purchased - Detail

The detail of the brands purchased survey provides in-depth segmentation purchase information. Basically, rather than providing a "slice" of information across brands, this report provides a summary of segmentation information for the market and a particular brand.

Base Cost:	Part of $100,000 Market Survey
Available:	Levels 2 & 3 only
Sort:	N/A
Graphs:	None
Next:	Displays the next brand listed in the Brands Purchased report

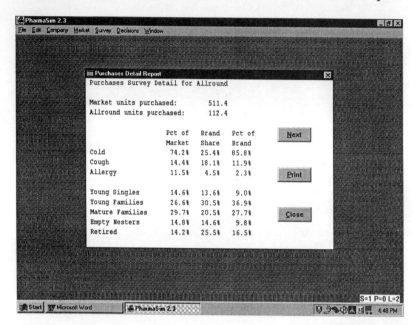

The top two lines of the report show the total units of cold related medication sold in the market during the past year and the total units sold for the selected brand. Dividing the brand units sold by the total market will calculate the overall market share for the brand that matches the Brands Purchased report.

The table in the second half of the report provides population, share, and percent of brand sales data for the selected product for each segment. To get intersection data (e.g. Young Singles who purchase allergy medication), the Brands Purchased report still must be used, but this report provides a helpful summary of information.

Percent of Market = The percent of total purchases made by a segment. In the screen above, 74.2% of OTC cold medication purchases were for cold usage, 14.4% for cough, and 11.5% for allergy. Likewise, Young Singles purchased 14.6% of all OTC cold medication and so on.

Brand Share = The share of units purchased for a brand in a particular segment. For instance, Allround has 25.4% share of cold sufferers and 13.6% share of young singles.

Percent of Brand = The percentage of the brand's total unit sales purchased by a particular segment. In the above example, 85.8% of Allround's sales come from cold sufferers and 36.9% come from Young Families. Each group (symptom/illness and stage of life) add to 100%.

Survey - Purchase Intentions

The market survey of purchase intentions displays what consumers were most likely to purchase before they actually enter the retail outlet. Often, the consumer will switch to a different brand due to price discount or other point of purchase promotions within the outlet. This survey will help determine if consumer promotion and/or pricing is making an impact on the consumer.

Base Cost:	Part of $100,000 Market Survey
Available:	Cross Section -- Levels 2 & 3
	Overall Only -- Level 1
Sort:	Yes
Graphs:	Cross Section of Purchase Intentions by Brand

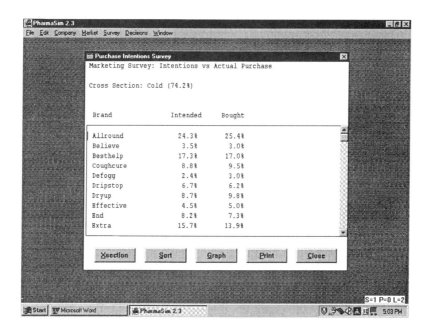

In the above example, Allround picks up significant sales while the consumer is in the store (25.4% purchases vs. 24.3% intentions). This is likely due to Allround's good shelf facings (shelf space) and in-store promotions. Note that this example is also showing cold sufferers segment rather than the overall market. In this report, as in the other market survey reports, any cross-section can be chosen for more segment specific information.

Survey - Satisfaction

The market survey report on consumer satisfaction estimates the percent of purchasers of each product who are satisfied with their product choice and are likely to repurchase. In PharmaSim, those who are satisfied are likely to be brand loyal rather than a "shopper". This survey is based on purchases, so heavy users are weighted more than light users.

Base Cost:	Part of $100,000 Market Survey
Available:	Cross Section -- Levels 2 & 3
	Overall Only -- Level 1
Sort:	Yes
Graphs:	Cross Section of Satisfaction by Brand

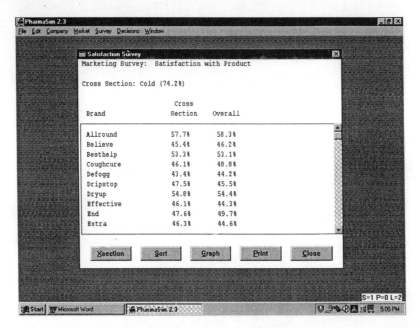

This report shows that 57.7% of cold sufferers are satisfied with the Allround brand. This is the highest among all brands and their 58.3% overall is also the best in the industry. This is a significant advantage for their product as both repurchases and word of mouth recommendations will be higher than other brands.

Survey - Brand Awareness

The market survey of awareness, trial, and repurchase indicates what percent of consumers are currently aware of a brand, have tried a brand, and purchase a particular brand most often. The conversion ratio shows the percent of those who are aware of a brand have tried it, while the retention ratio calculates the percent of those who have tried a brand who now purchase it most frequently.

Base Cost: Part of $100,000 Market Survey
Available: Cross Section -- Levels 2 & 3
                    Overall Only -- Level 1
Sort: Yes
Graphs: Cross Section of Awareness by Brand

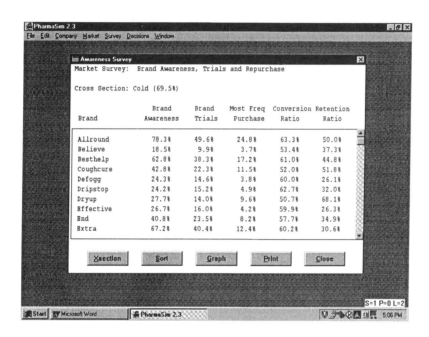

Conversion Ratio = Trials / Awareness, or of those aware of a brand, what percent have tried it.

Retention Ratio = Most Freq Purchased / Trials, or of those who have tried a brand, the percentage that purchase it most frequently.

Note that the cold sufferers now represent 69.5% of the market rather than 74.2%. This is because this study only counts each consumer once rather than taking into consideration usage. The difference is especially apparent on allergy sufferers.

Survey - Decision Criteria

The market survey of decision criteria indicates what factors are most important to the consumer's brand preference. The five factors considered are product effectiveness, side effects, price, form, and duration.

Base Cost:	Part of $100,000 Market Survey
Available:	Cross Section -- Levels 2 & 3
	Overall Only -- Level 1
Sort:	Yes
Graphs:	Cross Section of Average Rank of Decision Criteria

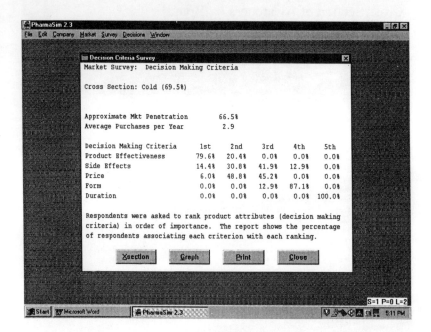

Market penetration is defined as the number percent of people in this cross-section who use medication to relieve a cold related symptom.

Average purchases per year are the purchases of cold medicine by the selected consumer segment. This is often referred to as usage.

Survey - Brand Perceptions

The market survey of brand perceptions summarizes consumer's opinions of a brand's effectiveness. The report compares the perceived strengths and weaknesses of a brand against various symptoms. Cross sections must be selected from the SEGMENTATION menu choice.

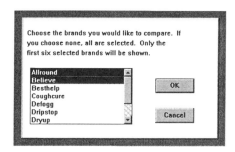

Select up to six brands to compare. Select <OK> to view the perceptual comparison similar to the example shown below:

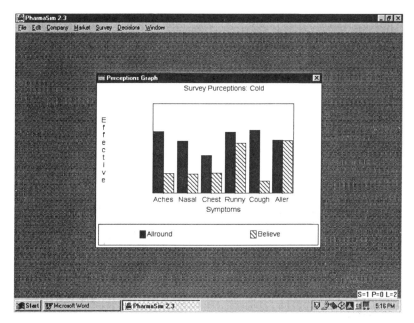

In the above example, the Allround brand is viewed as more effective than BestHelp against aches, chest congestion and cough but less effective against nasal congestion, runny nose and allergy symptoms. As manager for Allround, your firm might decide that the advertising message should be to improve Allround's perceived effectiveness against runny nose or nasal congestion (this detailed advertising message is only available at the brand manager level).

Survey - Trade-offs

The market survey of trade-offs shows how consumers make trade-offs between price and effectiveness. The line displayed at an angle across the grid represents their expected price for a given level of effectiveness. Each brand's perceived price and effectiveness is plotted in relation to this line. Higher priced brands are on the top part of the grid and brands with highest perceived effectiveness are on the right hand side of the grid. Cross sections must be selected from the SEGMENTATION menu choice.

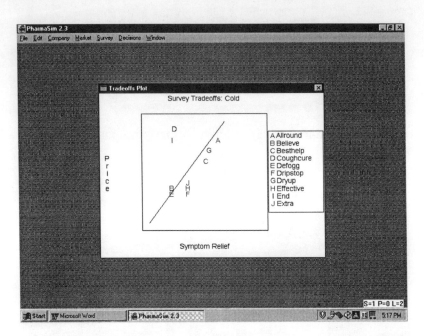

This report may be used to analyze a brand's "value" to the consumer. Those brands located below the line have a lower price than anticipated and therefore higher value. Those brands above the line are not as effective as consumers expect for their price. The location of brands and the trade-off line will vary considerably depending on the segmentation used. Attempt to recognize the different perceptions and needs for each segment selected.

Decisions - Level 1 (Brand Assistant)

There are five decision variables at level 1 ("Brand Assistant") -- Manufacturer suggested retail price, promotional allowance, promotional expenditures (consumer and trade), advertising expenditures, and sales force personnel (direct and indirect). All of the budgeted values are displayed in millions of dollars. There are two input screens to complete that are shown below.

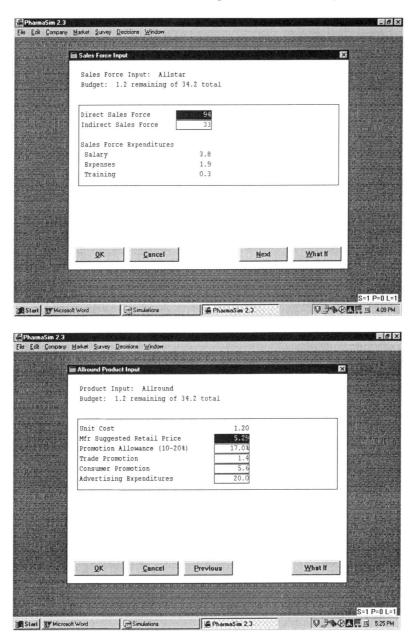

The sales force is divided into direct (account managers for channel customers) and indirect (wholesalers, merchandisers, detailers) employed during the coming year. The lines below that show the amount that will go to salary, expenses, and training. Each salesperson costs $30,000 in salary and $15,000 in expenses. A $10,000 training cost is incurred if the salesperson is new. Typically, sales force turnover runs between 10% and 20% each year. Keep in mind that new hires are not as effective as experienced personnel are.

The MSRP is only a guideline as to what retail outlets should charge for your brand. The actual price paid by the consumer will depend upon a number of other factors such as retail and wholesale markup, promotional allowance, and volume discount. At level 1, volume discounts are automatically calculated. The promotional allowance must be between 10% (the minimum allowance in order to gain shelf space) and 20% (the accepted industry maximum). Promotional expenditures represent all consumer and trade promotions such as point-of-purchase displays, co-op advertising, trial size mailings, and coupons. Advertising is total media expenditures for the coming year, including the cost of the advertising agency.

The available budget line displays the remaining budget. This must be greater than or equal to zero. If less than zero, the simulation cannot be advanced and expenditures must be cut. A message to this effect will be displayed when attempting to advance the simulation. Marketing research expenditures are included in the budget and these are accumulated as reports are accessed and purchased. The BUDGET ALLOCATION menu option displays a summary of how the budget is allocated across brands and marketing expenditures. A sample of this screen is displayed below.

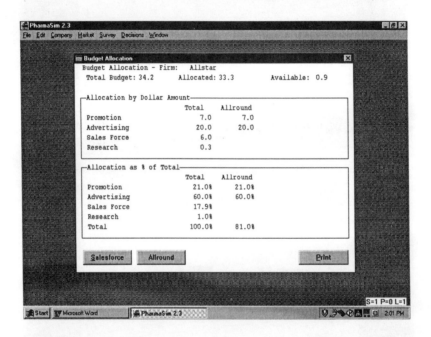

After entering decisions, it is a good idea to experiment with several "what if..." scenarios. Use the WHAT IF... menu item on the DECISIONS menu.

The WHAT IF... screen is an important financial check on decisions, especially pricing. It may also be used as a sensitivity or breakeven analysis on price and unit sales. However, it is up to you to determine whether the sales estimates are realistic. The default unit sales values are the unit sales from the previous period plus projected market growth. Thus, for a new product, this value would be zero. *The software makes no attempt to forecast sales based on your decisions on this screen.* Therefore, if significant changes are made which you believe will change your market share, you should adjust the sales estimate accordingly.

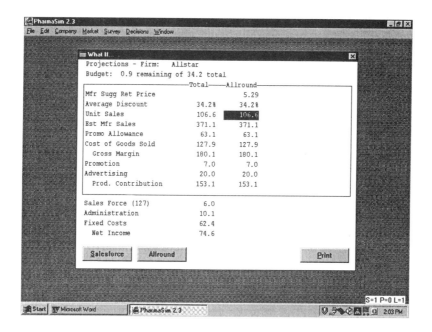

Any changes in price made on this screen will not alter your actual decisions. It is used only as a temporary calculation. In order to change prices, use the pricing decision screen.

Most of the values in the WHAT IF... analysis are taken directly from the decision screens. The average discount and promotional allowance are calculated using last year's sales patterns. Administration and fixed costs are calculated using the same method the simulation uses.

The other two options in the DECISION menu at level 1 will only be activated under certain circumstances. For your firm's first decision, neither option will be available. The ADD/CHANGE PRODUCT option is available whenever your firm has a new product, line extension, or reformulation option. Always check this menu choice first to see whether your firm has any important product mix decisions. The option to DISCONTINUE PRODUCT cancels a product line which is no longer beneficial to your company. This option will only be available when there are two or more products (or line extensions) in your portfolio. Both of these options have a significant impact on your strategy and performance. Please refer to the Reformulation and New Product Introduction part of this section for more information.

Decisions - Level 2 (Assistant Brand Manager)

At level 2 ("Assistant Brand Manager"), there is much greater control over marketing variables. Sales force may be allocated by channel and support function. Pricing adds volume and wholesaler discounts. Advertising now requires a description of the message in terms of primary, benefits, comparison, and reminder emphasis, as well as choice of an advertising agency. Promotion includes more detail in the type of consumer and trade promotion available.

Notice at level 2 that the menu structure has also changed. PRODUCT INPUT has been replaced with SALES FORCE, PRICING, ADVERTISING, and PROMOTION. Each brand on the market is now listed as a menu option. SALES FORCE has the sales force decisions, while the other three options contain the pricing, advertising, and promotion decisions for each particular brand. If multiple products are on the market (only an issue after period 3), make a particular brand active by selecting it from the DECISIONS menu. The four input screens at decision level 2 follow.

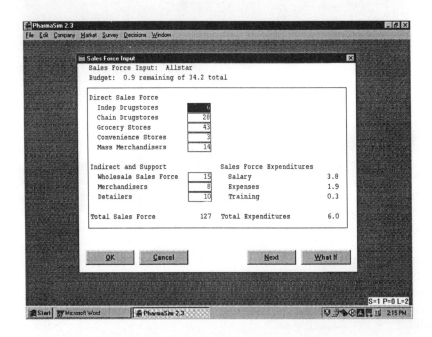

Direct sales force is the number of salespeople who sell to and support each direct sales channel. Wholesaler sales force is the number of people who support the wholesaler/indirect channel. Merchandisers are used as supplemental sales support and focus on channel activities such as checking on special promotions, improving shelf location, and other in-store support. The detailers attempt to influence physicians and pharmacists by distributing free samples and promotional material.

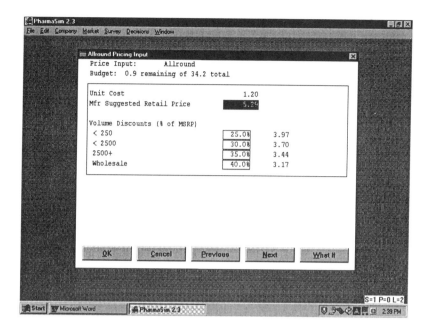

The input screen above is used to enter pricing and volume discounts. Enter a manufacturer suggested retail price, three volume discounts, and discount to the wholesaler. In all cases, the price to the wholesaler must be less than or equal to the volume discount prices, and larger volumes must be priced less than or equal to lower volumes. The industry standard discounts range from 15-30% for lower volumes to 20-45% for large volumes and wholesalers.

Typically, mass merchandisers and chain drugstores buy direct in large quantities, while independent drugstores normally use wholesalers. Grocery and convenience stores use both direct and wholesale channels.

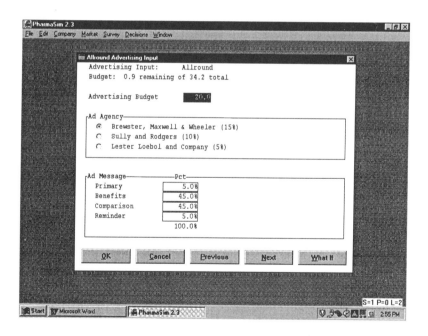

On the previous page is a sample input screen for advertising budget, message, and agency. The advertising budget is the total amount spent on media expenditures. Much of this budget goes toward network TV time slots. The selected advertising agency then takes a percentage of the total budget for their services. Each agency charges a different percentage for their services. The advertising message is determined by what percent your firm selects for primary, benefits, comparison, and reminder advertising.

Agency	Quality	Cost (% of media expend.)
Brewster, Maxwell and Wheeler (BMW)	High	15%
Sully & Rodgers (S&R)	Mid	10%
Lester Loebol & Company (LLC)	Low	5%

Message:		
Primary	- Creates awareness and stimulates primary demand
Benefits	- Emphasizes product benefits to consumer
Comparison	- Compares product with competitor
Reminder	- Maintains awareness and stimulates repurchase

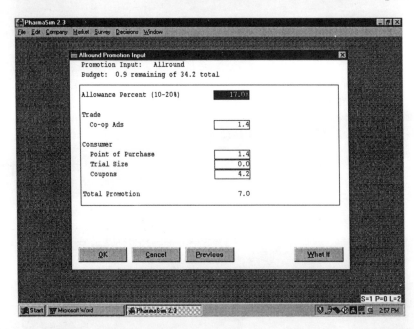

Promotional decisions include the promotional allowance, co-op ads, and consumer promotion. The promotional allowance is the percentage given to retailers for promotional expenditures. This value must be in the range from 10-20% and is basically seen as an additional price discount. The promotional budget is comprised of co-op advertising allowances, product/point-of-purchase displays, trial size promotions, and newspaper coupons.

Promotional Vehicles:

Promotional Allowance	- Gains shelf space and retailer promotion.
Co-op Advertising	- Helps retailers promote product. Improves awareness.
Point of Purchase Displays	- Attempts to create consumer brand switching at purchase.
Trial Size	- Generates trial and awareness.
Coupons	- Stimulates repurchase and trials among shoppers.

Use the < Next > and < Prev > buttons to move among input screens or use the menus.

Decisions - Level 3 (Brand Manager)

Level 3 ("Brand Manager") enhances advertising and promotion decisions. Please see level 2 decisions for the pricing and sales force input screens, as they remain unchanged at level 3. At level 3, advertising is now divided into two screens -- one for consumer targeting, another for the advertising message. Promotion is divided into consumer and trade promotion screens.

Use the target segments area to create an advertising message that appeals to certain demographic groups. For instance, if research shows that cough medicine was best suited for older people, mark the boxes "Empty Nesters," "Retired," and "Cough". This directs the advertising agency to create an ad theme which appeals to older people suffering from coughs, and air the ad at times when that target segment is most likely to be watching television.

Use the "compare with" section to target a certain competitor in your advertisement. Marking one of the competitive brands directs the advertising agency to create an ad that explains to consumers why your brand is better than the competitor's. This attempts to change consumer's perceptions of your brand's effectiveness versus a competitor's. This section uses the comparison % of ad message on the ad targeting section to determine how much emphasis to put on this type of advertisement. The higher the percentage, the more often comparative ads will be aired.

This "promote benefits" area is the final part of defining the advertising message. Each box marked in this section directs the advertising agency to specifically mention certain product qualities during the commercial. Again, the benefits % of ad message determines how many ads of this type will be aired.

In general, it is best to target your ad to some degree. For instance, it is fairly rare to see a commercial for a cough medicine that fails to at least mention the fact that it is for coughs. Also, it is rare to see children's cold medicine advertisements not mention that it is for children. In other words, tell potential consumers (target market) that your brand is best suited for them. The "compare with" and "promote benefits" messages attempt to change consumers' perception of your brand. Consumer perception of products may be analyzed by studying the market survey of brand perceptions (SURVEY - BRAND PERCEPTIONS).

A sample trade promotion input screen is shown below. For the promotion allowance, enter a value between 10% and 20% for each channel. Then select which channels may receive trade deals for co-op advertising.

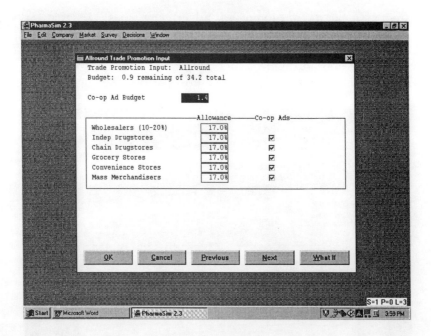

Consumer promotion decisions at level 3 include budget amounts for point of purchase, trial size and coupons. Select the channels that will receive point of purchase displays. Also remember to choose a coupon amount.

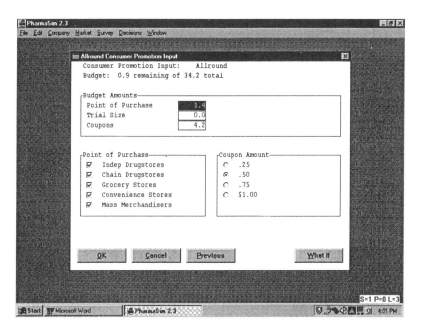

The additional options for promotion at level 3 allow targeting of specific channels of distribution. It is likely that some channels will be more receptive to particular forms of trade promotion than others. Consider using more resources where consumers are most likely to buy the product. For instance, if more people are likely to shop for cough medicine in independent drugstores it may make sense to target co-op ads and/or product displays for these types of distribution outlets.

Reformulation and New Product Introductions

At various times during the play of PharmaSim, product development will indicate that a brand reformulation or a new product is available for introduction. When this option becomes available, the ADD/CHANGE PRODUCT choice under the DECISIONS menu option is activated. There will also be a notification in the MARKETING UPDATE. When this menu choice is selected, a screen that outlines the basic product choices is displayed. Line extensions and new product introductions will receive additional budget funds. A general description and anticipated timing of these types of decisions are listed below:

End of period 1/   Allround reformulation. Choose between two slight modifications of the
Decisions for 2:   Allround brand or keep the same formulation.

End of period 3/   Line extension. Choose among three formulations for a line extension or
Decisions for 4:   choose not to introduce one.

End of period 5/   New product. Choose among three new product formulations, one of
Decisions for 6:   which is currently a prescription-only medication (with higher costs).

End of period 7/   Allround reformulation. Decide on your own formulation of the Allround
Decisions for 8:   brand.

The ability to reformulate Allround or introduce new products is available for two periods. The period listed above is when the reformulation option becomes available. For example, if Allround is not reformulated at the end of period 1, there will be another chance after period 2. Below is a sample reformulation screen.

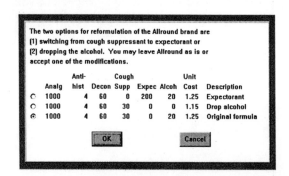

Discontinuing a Product

Once two or more brands are on the market, one may discontinue a product using DISCONTINUE PRODUCT under DECISIONS. This usually means that a brand is in a very sad state. However, it also may be that resources could be better utilized if focused on only one (or two) remaining products. When dropping a product, remember to take into account capacity considerations. Since production capacity cannot be decreased, hopefully another brand's increase in production will offset the brand that was dropped. In other words, all the fixed production costs are still being carried even after the brand is dropped. Since this is not in the product contribution statement, remember to take this into account when analyzing the financial implications of discontinuing a product line.

Section 3: Strategy and Tactics

PharmaSim is designed to be a realistic computer simulation. Allstar Brands, though quite profitable, has some long-term challenges ahead. The firm will likely go through both good times and bad. Competitors are making the types of decisions that might be expected in the "real world". In other words, they are not perfect, random, or inane.

There is no ultimate solution for PharmaSim. In fact, many different strategies, if followed consistently, can be quite profitable. Remember, the main goal while using PharmaSim is to learn. Throughout the course of the simulation, one should continually appraise the current situation. The markets, competitors, and environment are constantly changing. To be successful, one must not only thoroughly understand the current dynamics but also try to anticipate the future environment.

Below is a set of questions that should be considered while reviewing marketing research and making product decisions:

> Who are our current customers? What do they want?
> Who are our potential customers? What do they want?
> How is the market changing?
> Are there identifiable segments?
> Are there any segments whose needs are not being met by any current products?
> What competitive issues do we face?
> How is the environment changing?
> What are the current problems and opportunities?
> What are the long-term problems and opportunities?
> What are the financial implications of our decisions?
> What are our alternatives?
> How should we allocate our resources among brands?
> How should we allocate our resources across marketing functions?
> Which of our new product choices has the greatest potential for success?

This series of questions can be distilled into an overall decision making process as follows as shown in Exhibit 3.1.

In PharmaSim, this process should occur each period. The situation analysis and identification of problems and opportunities is derived from the firm results and marketing research. Alternative marketing plans should be generated based on group discussion (if played in a group situation) or careful individual consideration. Decisions are then entered and their feasibility is checked using the WHAT IF... analysis. Then the simulation is run, providing feedback on your decisions from the marketplace. At this point, of course, the process starts again from the beginning.

More detail on this process is given throughout this section. The discussion then shifts to some possible strategies and tactics you might use in the simulation. Along the way, you will find a number of "consulting tips" for those challenging times ahead.

Exhibit 3.1 - Suggested PharmaSim Decision Making Process

Situation Analysis:	Nature of demand, extent of demand, competitive dynamics, environment, cost structure, distribution structure, and financial resources.
Problems & Opportunities:	Identify key problem areas and key opportunities derived from the situation analysis.
Alternatives:	Generate a list of company and product/market objectives and marketing mix options based on your list of problems and opportunities.
Decision:	Choose the best alternative.
Monitor Results:	Are things going according to plan?

Situation Analysis - Nature of Demand

Understanding the nature of demand basically boils down to answering the question, "How do consumers make their purchase decisions?" To fully understand this process one should try to describe the buying behaviors and attitudes of the consumer. You may be able to use your own experiences to some degree, but do not impose your personal decision-making process on your target consumers. Try to find out what makes their decision or conclusion different from yours. Marketing research can be of great assistance in analyzing these behavior patterns. Below is a set of questions which may help you better understand their purchase decisions:

Questions	Where to find information in PharmaSim
What causes consumers to need the product?	MARKET - Symptoms Reported
What product attributes are important to the consumer?	SURVEY - Decision Criteria
	SURVEY - Tradeoffs
Are consumers aware of a particular brand?	SURVEY - Brand Awareness
Have consumers tried a particular brand?	SURVEY - Brand Awareness
Are consumers loyal to/satisfied with a particular brand?	SURVEY - Satisfaction
	SURVEY - Purchase Intentions
Where do consumers buy the product/brand?	MARKET - Shopping Habits
	MARKET - Share of Channel Sales
Who influences the decision maker?	MARKET - Recommendations
What are the actual attributes of brands?	MARKET - Brand Formulations
What are consumers' perceptions of brands?	SURVEY - Brand Perception

Once you have some general idea of how consumers make decisions, it is then important to find out if groups of consumers make decisions in a similar manner. Try to determine whether the market can be segmented or grouped based on "what they want" and "how they buy". One reason for doing this is to target your marketing resources at consumers with common needs and buying patterns. In most cases, this will lead to a more efficient use of your limited resources.

Some generally useful variables to consider for segmentation include: age, family life-cycle, geographic location, and product usage. Attitude based segmentation or consumer psychographics is another, and perhaps more insightful segmentation method. In PharmaSim, one has the ability to segment based on illness (product usage) and demographics (family life-cycle/age). This information is available under SURVEY - SEGMENTATION or through the <Xsection> button on most of the SURVEY reports. In any period of play, any of the SURVEY reports may be viewed based on any segmentation scheme. When viewing these reports, one should ask whether the information is significantly different using different segmentation schemes. Do all segments view your product in the same way? If not, why? Again, this should provide more insight into the purchase process of targeted consumers.

Finally, keep track of how the nature of demand changes over time. Consumers do not necessarily come to the same conclusion every time they make a purchase decision. Their needs may change, their information level may change, and the environment may change. It is important to try to anticipate how these dynamics evolve over time, and how this may affect marketing decisions.

Situation Analysis - Extent of Demand

This aspect of situation analysis attempts to determine the current and future size of the market in units and dollars. This information is important to assess what market opportunities offer the greatest potential. A smaller, high-growth market may offer more long-term advantages than a larger, stagnant market. In PharmaSim, one should analyze values on both an aggregate level (i.e. the total market for OTC cold medications) as well as a segmented basis (e.g. the market for children's cold medicine). The information is often used with an estimated market share to arrive at a forecast for unit and dollar sales (market size x share = units sold).

This information is in the PharmaSim marketing research under the following menu choices.

Total Retail Sales	= $1,996 million	From MARKET - Share of Channel Sales
Total Mfr Sales	= $1,491 million	From MARKET - Share of Mfr Sales
Total Unit Sales	= 511.4 million	From SURVEY - Brands Purchased <Detail>
Allround Unit Sales	= 102.1 million	From COMPANY - Product Contribution
Market Share (Units)	= 22%	From SURVEY - Brands Purchased

One other issue to consider is whether you are trying to measure the actual market (sales) or the potential market. For instance, actual sales for cold medicine might be 511 million units each year, however, it is likely that less than 100% of the people suffering from colds are buying medicine. The actual value might be closer to 60%. This value would be considered current market penetration. If market penetration increased from 60% to 80%, actual sales would climb significantly (33%).

Another related issue is average usage. If the average usage in the current market is 2.7 (i.e. each person who buys cold medicine uses an average of 2.7 bottles/year) what happens if usage increases to 3.0? Sales would climb 11%. Therefore, one should go beyond the basics of unit sales and also consider market penetration and usage when estimating market demand. Below are some questions which may help you better understand the extent of demand in a market:

Questions	Where to find information in PharmaSim
What is the current level of sales $?	MARKET - Share of Mfr Sales
	MARKET - Share of Channel Sales
What is the growth rate of sales?	Same two studies, but use graphs
What is the growth rate of the population?	MARKET - Industry Outlook
What is the approximate market penetration?	SURVEY - Decision Criteria
What is the average usage per year?	SURVEY - Decision Criteria
How many units of my brand were sold?	COMPANY - Product Contribution

Often the values for the total market are readily available, but segmented estimates are more difficult to calculate. The share of manufacturer sales (MARKET - SHARE OF MFR SALES) provides an estimate of cold, cough, allergy, and nasal spray sales in manufacturer dollars. However, you may prefer more defined segments. Also, remember that in the "Share of Mfr Sales" study, these "segments" are defined strictly by what label the manufacturer puts on the brand rather than a consumer's actual use. For instance, you may have a brand labeled as "cold" which is often used for allergies.

Given this, how might unit sales in a particular segment such as older cold sufferers be estimated? First, using the SURVEY - SEGMENTATION option, place an 'x' in front of "cold" and "retired". This selects the cross-section or segment to view. Then choose SURVEY - BRANDS PURCHASED and identify the percentage of the total population this segment represents. If this is 8.7%, then the market segment would be 44 million units/year (511 x .087 = 44).

Situation Analysis - Competitive Dynamics

Understanding the nature of your competition is critical to the success of any marketing plan. One must be able to anticipate (or at least be prepared for) possible competitor moves. Another benefit of truly understanding the competition is that through analysis of competitive marketing programs, one can often gain insight into what may be more effective use of marketing resources.

The final, and most difficult issue is anticipating the retaliatory moves your competitors may make, and whether or not they can neutralize your marketing programs. Specifically, one should consider the effect changes in a competitor's price, sales force, promotion, or advertising approach may have on the success of your strategy. Your firm may want to use the "what if..." analysis to calculate the possible financial impact of various scenarios. However, you will have to estimate the effect on unit sales, as this will not be estimated automatically.

On the following page is a series of questions which may help you better understand the competitive dynamics in a market:

Questions	Where to find information
What are current market shares?	MARKET - Share of Mfr Sales
	MARKET - Share of Channel Sales
	SURVEY - Brands Purchased
What are the competitors' product attributes?	MARKET - Brand Formulations
What are the financial resources of my competitors?	MARKET - Operating Statistics
What is the production capability of the competition?	MARKET - Operating Statistics
What are the current marketing programs?	MARKET - Sales Force
	MARKET - Advertising
	MARKET - Promotion

Situation Analysis - Environment

The environment can have an enormous impact on marketing programs. Health concerns, waste disposal, and energy shortages are just some examples of "environmental" factors which have completely altered industries and marketing programs. A good example was the demand during the late 1980's for oat bran products because of their apparent health benefits for cholesterol reduction. Over 100 different oat bran products were marketed during this time. Imagine the impact of a study showing that oat bran caused stomach cancer or had no effect on cholesterol (in fact, a study was released in 1990 which claimed that oat bran had no effect on cholesterol count.)

In PharmaSim, there are several environmental factors that your firm should consider. The demand for cold medicine is very much dependent on the number of people reporting various illnesses, as well as seasonal influences (e.g. increased occurrence of influenza or high pollen count). There may be some underlying changes in health concerns that may be monitored by tracking physician recommendations or decision criteria of purchasers. In addition, the effect of inflation on costs and pricing should also be taken into consideration.

Situation Analysis - Cost Structure

The cost of manufacturing and selling a product can usually be broken into those variable and fixed costs. Examples of variable costs are direct materials, direct labor, packaging, and direct selling costs. In other words, costs which vary depending of the level of production or sales. Examples of fixed costs are plant, equipment, and administrative overhead. These are costs that remain fixed without regard to the level of production or sales. Understanding how these two costs interact is extremely important to the financial success of your firm. Consider the two extreme cases of 100% fixed versus 100% variable. How might your pricing and/or marketing strategy differ?

In the situation where all costs are variable, pricing is often done on a cost plus basis. For instance, the cost for producing and selling a good is $20/unit. If these are sold for $30, the company's margin on the unit is simply price (or sales) less variable costs, or $10/unit. Since there are no fixed costs, profit would also be $10.00 / unit. Breakeven in this case is at zero units.

Example - all variable costs:

Price	$30.00
Variable Cost (VC)	$20.00
Margin per unit sold	$10.00
Fixed Costs (FC)	$0.00

Breakeven (BE) = Fixed Costs / Margin per unit sold = $0.00 / $10.00 = 0 units
Additional profit generated for each unit sold = $10.00

However, determining where total profits are maximized is much more difficult. This is dependent on the number of units sold at various price points. Therefore, one would attempt to maximize (UNITS) * (PRICE - VC). By increasing units or price, or decreasing variable cost, profits will increase. Typically, as price increases, unit sales decrease (there are many examples of where this is not the case, such as Rolex watches, some luxury cars, services, or where price may be used as an indicator of quality). This is a trade-off one must attempt to understand as best as is possible.

On the other hand, if all costs are fixed, each unit sold contributes additional margin equal to the price of the good. Here the profit equation is (UNITS * PRICE) - FC. Notice how much more profit an additional unit of sales brings. Thus, firms with high fixed costs and low variable costs will often spend more marketing dollars in order to increase sales.

Example - all fixed costs:

Price	$30.00
Variable Cost (VC)	$ 0.00
Margin per unit sold	$30.00
Fixed Costs	$3000.00

Breakeven = Fixed Costs / Variable Margin 3000 / 30 = 100 units
Additional profit generated for each unit sold = $30.00

Another helpful way to analyze the financial implications of decisions is to calculate the number of units that need to be sold in order to generate some profit target. This equation would be as follows:

$$\text{Units to cover profit target} = \frac{\text{Profit target}}{(\text{Price} - \text{VC})} + \text{Breakeven units}$$

Of course, most situations involve an analysis of a number of marketing variables. A generalized profit equation that captures the relationship among these variables is:

Profit = (Total Market * Mkt Share) * (Price - Var. Costs) - (Fixed Costs + Mktg)

OR

Profit = Units Sold * Margin - (Overhead + Marketing)

Therefore, profit increases when the total market, market share, or price increases; or when variable costs or overhead decrease. Although there is nothing magical about this analysis, companies often mismanage the margin. If the focus is only on increasing sales (often through decreasing price to achieve greater market share), the margin will erode. It is also very easy for a competitor to match your price (unless there is a significant cost advantage for your firm). Thus, when you are considering lowering price, consider how many more units will need to be sold in order to generate the same profit. If fixed costs are high and variable costs are low, this may be a reasonable conclusion. If variable costs are significant, make sure to think through the reasoning. A better approach to increasing market share may be through an improved marketing program or product offering.

One final issue regards the definition of fixed costs. Fixed costs are typically defined as those costs that remain constant over a given range of production/sales volume. Fixed costs are very likely to change beyond this range. For instance, in PharmaSim, the major fixed cost item is the plant and equipment used for manufacturing capacity. This is constant until capacity increases (when demand > current capacity). Thus, be careful when capacity utilization approaches 100%. There will be a significant change in fixed costs when capacity increases. Using the WHAT IF... analysis may help show the effects of different prices and unit volumes. This analysis will include any changes in fixed costs. This analysis can also be used to estimate breakeven volume at a given price. Enter the price, then change the units sold value until profit equals zero. This is the breakeven volume.

Situation Analysis - Distribution Structure

The distribution structure of an industry plays an important role in marketing decisions. In some industries, manufacturers sell direct to the consumer, while in others there are multiple levels of distribution (brokers, wholesalers, retailers, etc.). It is important to understand the role of each channel member, their strengths, and their needs. Typically, as more intermediaries come between the manufacturer and the consumer, the amount of control the manufacturer has in the marketplace decreases. In addition, the manufacturer may not receive important market feedback directly from the consumer. This points to the need for marketing research. Some of the issues concerning distribution are summarized below.

Questions	Where to find information in PharmaSim
What is the ultimate point of purchase?	MARKET - Share of Retail Sales
What role do intermediaries play?	MARKET - Industry Outlook
What are channel policies regarding markup?	MARKET - Pricing
What channels are frequented by our target consumers?	MARKET - Shopping Habits
Are we receiving adequate channel support?	MARKET - Shelf Space

Much of the information regarding channel policies (markup, use of wholesalers, needs, etc.) is found in the case at the beginning of this manual. It is extremely important to understand the needs of the individual channel in terms of discounts, allowances, support, and turnover.

Situation Analysis - Financial Resources

Throughout the course of the simulation, financial resources are limited. This is administered in the game through the use of a budget, similar to one a brand manager might have. The budget is based partly on last period's budget, partly on current results (net income), and partly on need (additional budget is allocated for new product introductions). The minimum budget is $20 million, even if financial performance indicates further cuts might be appropriate.

It is critical to understand how to generate the profit necessary to meet your investment objectives. Prices must create a margin that can sustain administrative overhead, fixed costs, and marketing expenditures. If the margin erodes without any corresponding increase in volume, you may find that marketing expenditures must be cut to meet budget. Since fixed costs cannot be decreased, and administrative overhead cannot be lowered dramatically, marketing expenditures will be the first to go. As the ability to promote and advertise products is lost, sales may soon follow suit. This is a difficult downward spiral to overcome.

Problems and Opportunities

At some point during the simulation, problems will arise. Issues such as competitors' new product introductions, financial constraints, over-capacity, or competitor's marketing programs may cause these problems. It is important to distinguish between a problem and a symptom. A symptom is the obvious result from a problem. For instance, you may see that sales or profits are down. You have identified a symptom. Now you need to diagnose what real problem caused this symptom. Keep asking "why" until the root problem is found. An example:

Situation	Profits are down	Symptom

| Why? | Sales are down | Symptom |
| Why? | Market share is down | Symptom |

| Why? | Competitor product launch | Problem |

In many cases, a general symptom such as "profits are down" is caused by more than one problem. For instance, in the above example, it also might be that total market sales are down which compounds the downturn in product sales. The root "problem" here might be due to fewer colds reported because of a light flu season. (As you can see, marketers develop a warped view of the world once they realize that sales go up when people get sick). In any case, make sure you fully analyze the root causes of any symptom.

In PharmaSim, there are usually two types of crises: Financial ("My budget keeps getting lower" or "my net income is negative"), and the sometimes related sales performance ("No one is buying my product" or "my market share falls every year").

Financial crises, when not combined with sales problems, are often caused by failure to understand the cost structure of your firm or product. Often, using a low price strategy to gain market share (or slow the decline) will erode your gross margin. You need to make sure that your gross margin is sufficient to cover your firm's budget costs and fixed costs. If not, your net contribution will suffer. Another common cause for financial distress is severe under-utilization of capacity. If your firm is saddled with large fixed costs as a percent of sales because of idle plants, it will be difficult to be profitable. Carefully analyze costs as a percent of sales compared to the competition. If some of your values are significantly higher, you need to find out why. For a more thorough description of cost issues, please see the cost structure discussion earlier in this section.

Sales crises are typically more difficult to diagnose. Usually, the problem boils down to either a product or a marketing mix issue.

Product Related Issues	Where to find information in PharmaSim
Poor product formulation	MARKET - Brand Formulations
	MARKET - Recommendations
	SURVEY - Brand Awareness (retention)
	SURVEY - Satisfaction
Product doesn't match needs of consumer	SURVEY - Decision Criteria
Poor product effectiveness	SURVEY - Tradeoffs
Poor product perception	SURVEY - Brand Perception

Marketing Mix Related Issues	
Pricing out of line with perceived value	SURVEY - Tradeoffs
Low awareness or trials	SURVEY - Brand Awareness
Not receiving enough shelf space	MARKET - Shelf Space
Targeting wrong segment	SURVEY - Segmented Reports
Ad message not consistent with product stage	MARKET - Advertising
Trade or consumer promotion not effective	COMPANY - Promotion report

There is not a great deal of control over specific product formulations in PharmaSim. When the option of a reformulation or new product launch becomes available, the key is to choose the product that has the best opportunity for success in the market. After the launch the goal becomes concentrating on finding consumers who will want your product and convincing them to buy it. Support of the wholesalers and retail outlets is essential because channels of distribution and point of purchase are such important aspects of this industry. Many consumers make brand decisions while in the store. Therefore your firm must maintain adequate shelf space through sufficient trade promotion and sales force. Issues such as shelf space and consumer awareness are especially important in new product introductions. It is a fairly simple fact that if consumers are not aware of your brand or cannot find your brand, they will not buy your brand. Of course, even if consumers are aware and shelf space is reasonable, your sales will suffer if you have the wrong product.

Discovering problems in your targeting strategy or advertising message is more difficult. You may have to compare results in your target segments from one period to the next to see if your marketing plan is effective. Defining the correct advertising message requires both understanding the needs of your product at its current stage (introductory, growth, maintain, decline), as well as analyzing competitor messages.

Opportunities

Along with focusing on fixing problems, it is also important to find and assess new opportunities. An obvious opportunity exists in PharmaSim when the option to introduce a new product or reformulate an existing brand becomes available. Yet there are many other opportunities such as discovering new market trends, having the ability to use new marketing variables (when you increase your level of play), or being able to take advantage of a competitor's mistake. When you note an opportunity, do not immediately decide whether your firm should act, but instead define the opportunity well and assess its value. The better the definition of the opportunity, the better the ability to shape marketing plans to take advantage of that opportunity.

Alternatives

Once you have done a thorough situation analysis and compiled a list of problems and opportunities, put together a series of marketing program alternatives for your brands. A marketing program consists of a set of decisions regarding marketing mix variables that helps achieve some goal. A marketing program that makes sense for one product will not necessarily work for another product. Often different marketing programs are needed for different target segments using the same product. A general outline for discussing marketing program issues is described below:

1. Define your objectives

    a. Target market segments
    b. Volume to be sold / market share
    c. Profit analysis (contribution, breakeven, ROI, etc.)

2. Marketing mix / program alternatives

    a. Product decisions (add new products, change products, drop products)
    b. Distribution decisions (channels to target, use of wholesalers)
    c. Pricing decisions (MSRP, discounts)
    d. Sales force decisions (budget, direct and indirect allocation)
    e. Advertising decisions (media expenditures, message, agency)
    f. Promotional decisions (allowances, trade and consumer promotion mix)

3. Budget check (Do we have the funds?)

4. Anticipate competitive response

    a. How will other firms respond to your plan?
    b. What are the competitors' resources?
    c. Can competitors neutralize your plan?
    d. Anticipate timing of responses

It is essential that all aspects of your marketing mix alternative be consistent with each other, as well as with your objectives. While you are generating an alternative plan, consider the pros and cons of each aspect.

Decisions

If you have performed a thorough analysis and have a guiding strategy, decisions are relatively easy. Although there may be several alternative programs, typically one will stand out as "feeling" better. This is usually when your experience comes into play. As each period goes by, you will gain more experience as to what makes a successful strategy in the PharmaSim world. You should neither ignore these "feelings" based on experience, nor let them lead your analysis. If they are not backed up with solid analysis, your feelings may be misleading or result in poor judgements. If your analysis focuses on finding data to back up your opinion, you will more than likely overlook other good possibilities.

> The best decisions are made when your experience agrees with your analysis.

Monitor Results

Once you have made your decisions and advanced the simulation, the next step is comparing your estimate of results (sales, market share, net income, etc. from a printout of your what if... analysis) with actual results. If there is a significant deviation, you should find out why. Sometimes results will be better than expected. Other times (and probably more often), results will be less than you hoped. Use downturns as motivation to understand the market better.

At this point, the process starts again. Update the situation analysis to include the most recent market developments, find the new problems and opportunities the market has created, and hash out a new set of alternative plans of action. Above all, though, have fun and learn. Remember, you usually have the option of re-running the simulation and trying different strategies and tactics (depending on the administrator's wishes).

Strategy and Tactics

The reason a discussion of strategy and tactics follows the decision-making process is that sound strategy and effective tactics are derived from a thorough understanding of the market and the competition. Short-term decisions must fit into a long-term strategy or vision for your company. Your corporate objective may be to increase profits, sales, and market share. This is typically where everyone starts. However, those objectives must be expanded into a corporate direction that will guide your strategy, and ultimately into short-term tactics to effectively implement your strategy.

Initially, your firm's strategy must center on the Allround brand. It is currently the most powerful brand name in the over-the-counter cold medicine market. More people buy Allround than any other brand, and its recognition and trial rate is higher than all other cold medicines. Allround has the added advantage of being used as an alternative to cough medicine for more serious coughs, and for coughs combined with cold symptoms. Because of Allround's strengths and its multi-symptom formulation, your company has been able to maintain an above average price without sacrificing unit sales. By focusing on delivering "value" to the customer, the brand has been extremely profitable for your company.

Recently, Allround's market share has slowly eroded because of new multi-symptom product introductions, such as the Dryup brand from Driscol. Other companies are expected to introduce new brands in the coming years, which may well further erode Allround's market position. Therefore, one of your goals for the Allround brand should be to combat this market erosion, and maintain share and sales volume. One possibility under consideration is a product reformulation for introduction in period 2 (decision to be made in period 1). It is important, however, that profitability is not sacrificed to maintain market share. Your firm may need the cash generated by a successful brand to help support a possible line extension introduction for period 4 (decision to be made in period 3).

According marketing analysts, one benefit of a line extension is the initial brand recognition (awareness) due to association with the Allround brand name. Line extensions may be used to target specific types of users; such as children, people who prefer tablets, or cough sufferers. This is viewed as a pro-active measure to secure market segments where the Allround brand might be susceptible to a well-targeted brand. One concern for the line extension is the problem of "cannibalism". It is possible that a significant portion of the buyers of your line extension will be people who would have bought the Allround brand in the first place. Developing a marketing program that minimizes this effect should be a priority.

Cannibalism will not be much of an issue for the new brand introduction slated for period 6 (decision made at the end of period 5). Here, your firm will be able to target specific users whose needs are not currently being met by existing brands. The introduction of a new brand calls for a much more extensive marketing plan. It is essential to generate brand awareness and trials, gain access to channels, and convince consumers to buy your brand. A successful brand introduction will require a marketing plan that is well planned and consistently implemented.

Throughout the course of the simulation there will be a number of issues that must be thoroughly understood and managed. Five of the most important are briefly discussed below, along with some tactical advice.

Targeting segments: When targeting specific demographic or product use groups, it is important to have a marketing plan that is consistent with the needs of the target group. This is especially important for the line extension and the new product introduction, as these are more likely to be marketed to a specific group. The advertising message should appeal to the target group and promote the benefits that are most important to them. When comparing with another brand, it makes sense to target current leader in that segment. This will create an advertising campaign that communicates why your brand is superior to the competing brand. The promotional strategy should be consistent with the overall brand strategy. Sales force and promotional allowances should favor those channels where the target segment buys products. Finally, pricing should take into account not only product costs, but also consumer sensitivity to pricing. For instance, if the target segment lists price as the most important factor in their brand decision, a low price approach may not only be more effective, but even necessary.

Pricing and costs: As mentioned above, the pricing decision should consider the price sensitivity of your target segments (or of the market overall). However, when using a low price strategy, do not forget to consider costs. First, calculate your margin for each unit sold. This would be MSRP - volume discounts - promotional allowance - cost of goods sold. This can be done automatically for you in the WHAT IF... analysis section. Second, calculate how many units are necessary to sell to cover advertising and promotion for that brand. Remember to factor in sales force and fixed costs that must be shared by all brands. Third, calculate the unit sales necessary to achieve a profit target. Ask yourself if this level is realistic given the entire marketing plan. Experiment with the profit sensitivity given various sales and pricing levels. Finally, remember that lowering price only gives you a temporary competitive advantage unless your company truly has lower costs than the competition. Competitors can quickly match your price and negate your temporary advantage.

Distribution: Understanding the needs of your distribution channels is an essential part of any well thought out marketing plan. For instance, when trying to gain prime shelf space in grocery stores, it is necessary to find out what is most important to these retail outlets. Refer to the case to find out what they consider when allocating shelf space among brands. Typically, retailers will consider stock turnover rates (brand sales volume), profitability, promotional allowances, sales support (sales force), and trade promotion. If shelf space for your brand is low in the target channels, sales will suffer. Since brand decisions for cold medicines are often made in the store, brands that are at eye level or have special point of purchase displays usually have an advantage over those brands found on the bottom shelf. Do not neglect your distribution channels.

Product Perceptions: Although your firm will no doubt believe that your brand is by far the most effective cold medicine, consumers may have a different opinion. Sometimes you will find that although one brand actually has more of a particular active ingredient which is effective against a symptom, another brand may be considered more effective. This is because people's perceptions of products are not always in line with the product's actual attributes. Advertising, influencers, brand loyalty, and misconceptions all play a role in shaping peoples' perception of a product. Typically, the best method of changing a brand's perceptions is through advertising. Advertising themes (message) which communicate product benefits or compare product attributes with a competitor's brand are the most effective method of changing the consumer's perception of a brand. Obviously, how other companies advertise their brands will affect your perceptions as well.

Brand loyalty: One method of building a sustainable competitive advantage is through increasing brand loyalty. Often in a packaged goods industry such as cold medicine, the usual purchase decision for a consumer is to simply buy the same brand they bought last time. Thus, established brands typically try to reinforce this behavior while new brands attempt to change it. Reminder advertising and the use of coupons are the two tools most often used to increase repurchases. Product displays, trial size promotions, and coupons are usually used to generate brand switching. In addition, pricing decisions, inherent consumer loyalty, and brand satisfaction have a significant affect on repurchase behavior.

Conclusion

PharmaSim has been designed to reward those players who perform a thorough market and competitive analysis and develop marketing plans that are:

    (1) customer focused,
    (2) reasonable in both the short- and long-term,
    (3) consistent and integrated,
    (4) financially sound, and
    (5) responsive to competitive strategies.

If you follow these guidelines, your firm will likely have an extremely prosperous ten years. Enjoy your tenure as a member of the Allstar brand management team.

Some parts of this chapter are based on an outline found in Cases in Marketing Management, 4th Edition, Bernhardt/Kinnear pp. 10-16. Published by Business Publications Inc. 1988.

Section 4: Resource Allocation Issues

At the start of the simulation, there is only one brand to manage. However, as the game progresses and line extensions and new brands are introduced, the issue of how to allocate a limited budget among brands becomes extremely important. This section introduces the concept of portfolio analysis, and describes several models used as a basis for allocating resources.

As you read this chapter, think about the role of each of your brands in PharmaSim. Ask yourself what role the Allround brand plays in the introduction of line extensions or new brands. How do the investment needs of brands influence the budget allocation process?

Introduction

In the example below, a division has four brands currently on the market. Sales, brand contribution, current market share, market share of the largest competitor, and market growth are listed for each brand. The division has a marketing budget of $20 million. Based on this information, how would you allocate the division's budget?

Exhibit 4.1: Example data from a division with four brands on the market

	Last Yr. Budget	Sales	Contri- bution	Market Share	Comp. Share	Market Growth	New Budget
Brand A	$ 10.0	$ 75.2	$ 15.6	18.3%	16.5%	2.1%	_____
Brand B	0.5	12.1	1.1	2.0%	22.3%	4.5%	_____
Brand C	8.0	172.5	3.7	27.3%	14.9%	16.2%	_____
Brand D	1.5	45.8	4.8	6.3%	12.5%	18.5%	_____

Although the information presented here is limited, you probably had some initial thoughts on an approach you might take. For instance, you might choose to keep the budget the same as last year. Often, budgets are primarily based on last year's budget. However, you might want to consider some other options such as sales or contribution. In other words, brands that have the highest sales or contribution will receive the highest budget. Some straightforward methods of allocating the budget lead to an interesting range of values and these are presented in Exhibit 4.2:

Each one of the example budget allocation approaches shown in Exhibit 4.2 has some merit. What is important to note is the wide range of outcomes possible based on simple allocation approaches. Obviously, it is the job of the division manager to sort out priorities, potential, and risks to arrive at an allocation decision.   But how does one go about evaluating market opportunities and cash allocation needs?

Exhibit 4.2: Various allocation methods applied to data from Exhibit 4.1.

Total budget to allocate = $20 Million

Basis for Allocation	Brand A	Brand B	Brand C	Brand D
Last Year's Budget	$ 10.0	$ 0.5	$ 8.0	$ 1.5
Sales	4.9	0.8	11.3	3.0
Contribution	12.4	0.9	2.9	3.8
Return on Expenditures	4.2	6.0	1.2	8.6
Market Size	1.3	3.1	13.0	2.7
Market Growth	1.0	2.2	7.8	9.0
Market Share	6.8	0.7	10.1	2.3
Relative Market Share				
(Your share / largest comp.)	6.3	0.5	10.4	2.9
Range	1.0 - 12.4	0.5 - 6.0	1.2 - 13.0	1.5 - 9.0

Example calculation for budget allocation based on sales:

Brand A represents 24.6% of the division's sales (75.2 / 305.6). Therefore, if budget were allocated based on sales, the brand would receive 24.6% of $20 million, or $4.9 million.

Strategic Business Units

A strategic business unit, or SBU, is any organizational group that has a unique set of customers, competitors, and definable costs. In a brand management firm, an SBU is often considered a brand or group of related brands. In other companies, an SBU is linked more with a target market than a product. For instance, a company might be organized by industry (banking, scientific, etc.). Ultimately, SBUs should be designed around product/markets that have the need for similar marketing or competitive strategies.

Question: How would you define SBUs in PharmaSim? Should each brand be an SBU or do you think the entire OCM group would be considered an SBU by management? Is this decision dependent on the point of view of the decision-maker?

Portfolio analysis is probably best used at this SBU level. However, the concepts and frameworks of resource allocation models are applicable at many levels in a business. Corporate resources may be allocated among divisions, and product resources are likely to be allocated across markets. The basic long-term goal in all of these models is to help managers better understand their businesses and improve their strategic decision-making ability. Short-term, the models can prove to be an invaluable aid in assessing SBU cash needs and cash generation.

The heart of the issue of resource allocation is that each SBU uses and generates cash, typically in different magnitudes. If SBUs are seen as independent units, investment decisions are made solely in the context of the alternatives open to that particular unit. However, when viewed in a corporate context, some SBUs may offer better investment alternatives than others. It is therefore important that those SBUs which are generating cash and which have poor investment options give their cash to units which are cash poor but have good investment alternatives. Typically, investment is usually needed to fund SBUs in higher growth markets, whereas cash is usually generated in low growth, high market share SBUs. This is the basis for the BCG growth-share matrix.

The BCG Growth-Share Matrix

In the 1960's the Boston Consulting Group (BCG) developed a model based on their analysis of the experience curve (see Exhibit 4.3) that summarized a business' market position. The matrix is probably the most widely used portfolio model, mainly because it is simple in its application. The model is based on the premise that growth rate is the best indicator of a market's attractiveness, and that relative market share (your share / largest competitor's share) is the best measure of a firm's strategic position in a market. This is because high relative market share leads to higher cumulative experience, which should result in lower costs and higher profits than competitors with lower relative market share. Since both market growth and market share are usually known to a manager, a BCG matrix can be constructed relatively quickly. The basic BCG framework is illustrated in Exhibit 4.4.

Exhibit 4.3 - The Experience Curve

The phenomenon of the experience curve is well documented in a number of industries. The basic premise is that as cumulative production increases there will be a corresponding decrease in unit cost. The function that is associated with the experience curve states that with each doubling of production, unit costs will decrease by roughly a fixed percentage. Thus, if unit costs at 100,000 units of cumulative production are $100 and the experience curve rate is 80%, unit costs at 200,000 units would be approximately $80. As cumulative production reaches 400,000 units, costs would decrease to about $64.

There are a number of factors that contribute to the experience curve effect. These include:

* Workforce related factors - such as productivity gains through worker job experience. As workers repeatedly do similar tasks, increases in efficiency often result. Workforce organization, employee training, worker effort, and management pressure also have a role in reducing costs over time.

* Process modifications - These include improvements in operations or inventory control, reduction of waste and production bottlenecks, and substitution of capital for labor or investment in new equipment.

* Actual changes in production technology that reduce costs.

* Product redesign and materials substitution. By modifying a product's design or components, significant cost savings can be gained through more efficient production processes or lower materials costs. Often product performance can also be improved at the same time.

It should also be noted that the experience curve effect is not automatic. Management and workers must actively participate in the cost reduction process.

The vertical axis represents market growth. The horizontal line that divides the matrix is often placed at market growth about equal to the growth of the economy as a whole or somewhat higher. Many companies use 10% as an arbitrary mid-point. The reasons that market growth is used as one of the main axes include:

1. Typically, it is easier to gain share in a high growth market and competitive rivalry is somewhat lower.

2. Higher growth markets are usually less price competitive because demand often exceeds supply.

3. Market growth is often used as an indicator of the stage in the product life cycle. Thus, low growth will often be considered a mature market, negative growth a declining market, and so on. The stage of the product life cycle will likely play a role in the manager's decision making process as well. Thus, the BCG matrix can quickly show an overview of where various SBUs stand in their life-cycle.

Exhibit 4.4 - The BCG Growth-Share Matrix

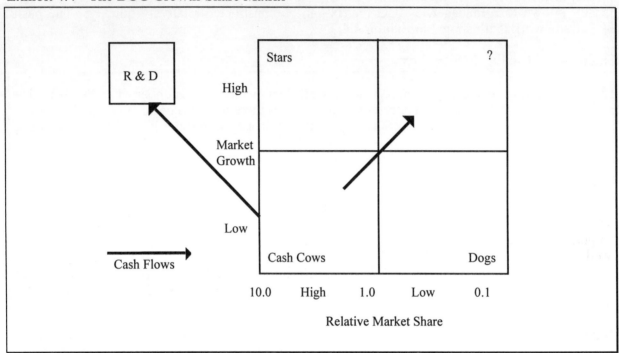

The horizontal axis of the BCG matrix represents relative market share where the midpoint is 1.0 (where your firm has the same market share as the other leading competitor). Often .80 is used to indicate that a strong secondary position in a market is still considered a "market leader". There are two basic reasons why relative market share was chosen as a main axis:

1. A firm with a relative market share of greater than 1.0 will move down the experience curve at a faster rate and thereby gain a long-term cost advantage.

2. A number of studies suggest that long-term profitability is related to market share. The best known studies are based on the PIMS (Profit Impact of Market Strategy) database which includes 1200 SBUs from over 200 firms.

Each of the four quadrants of the BCG matrix represents a predicted cash flow position. These quadrants have been descriptively labeled with the names: stars, question marks, dogs, and cash cows. Each SBU is then placed in the matrix according to its relative market share and market growth rate. Typically, the SBU is designated by a circle that corresponds to the relative size of sales. Thus, the SBUs with the highest sales are labeled with the largest circles. A BCG matrix for the example data presented earlier in this section is displayed in Exhibit 4.5.

Exhibit 4.5 - BCG Matrix Applied to Example Data

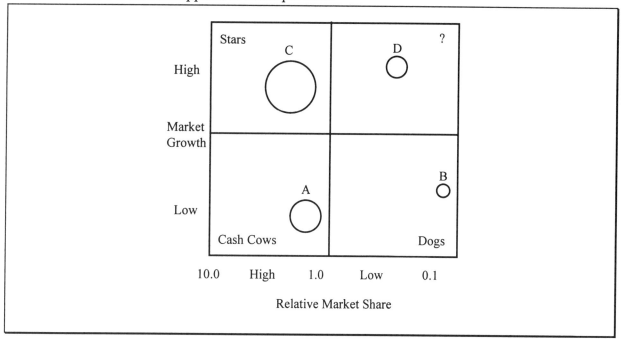

Cash Cows (the lower left - brand A) are SBUs in low-growth or mature markets with high share. Typically, they have a low cost position due to the experience effect, which allows them to generate significant cash flow for the organization. Sales volume is usually near its peak as well. Since the market is mature, cash investment needs are usually significantly lower and generate a positive net cash flow. The funds generated by cash cows should be used to move question marks to stars, to fund R&D projects, or to improve the competitive position of existing stars.

Stars (the upper left - brand C) are SBUs in high-growth markets with high share. These SBUs are expected to use a significant amount of funds to maintain share in a high-growth market. However, they should also provide large cash flows. In general, stars are usually close to self-supporting. It is important that cash flow is not siphoned from these SBUs sacrificing their long-term position. As market growth slows entering the mature phase, these stars should become cash cows. Thus, every attempt should be made to maintain or increase market share for stars, as these are the SBUs that are essential to the long-term success of your company.

Question Marks (the upper right - brand D) are SBUs in high-growth markets with lower share. These SBUs typically use large amounts of cash to fund their growth, but generate little cash because of their poor market position. Unless their market position is improved, they will likely end up as dogs when the market matures. Some question marks can be converted to stars depending on the market and competitive situation. Increasing market share in a growing market will normally require large amounts of cash.

Dogs (the lower right - brand B) are SBUs in low-growth markets with low share. Cash flow for these SBUs is typically low, or even negative. Because market growth is low, it is expected that it will take significant resources to change their competitive position. Unfortunately for most companies, dogs usually outnumber any other SBU classification. In some cases, dogs can become profitable by using a niche strategy and attempting to dominate a particular sub-segment of a market. This, in effect, redefines their market to where they have an improved competitive position. The other options for dogs include implementing a harvest strategy to generate cash, or selling the businesses.

When considering options for dogs, one should be careful to avoid poorly designed turn-around plans which often waste cash better invested in SBUs with greater potential. Another issue to consider is how a dog may impact other SBUs. For instance, a dog may in fact make many hidden contributions to overall success, such as helping to cover corporate overhead or supporting expensive technology development. Remember to consider these in your strategy formulation.

Assumptions of the BCG matrix

Although there are a number of issues that make over-reliance on the BCG matrix dangerous, two assumptions should be restated because of their importance to portfolio analysis and competitive theory in general. First, since competitive advantage built through dominant market share is based on achieving a low cost position through the experience curve (i.e. that an SBU will build a cost advantage over time with higher cumulative production than its competitors), it is essential that the experience curve is present in the industry and firm. One must also take into consideration other cost advantages a firm or competitor might possess which would lessen or negate the advantage due to the experience curve.

The second basic assumption concerns the definition of product/markets (and therefore, shares of those markets). Often, it is possible to define a market so narrowly that your firm will have dominant share. For instance, a local manufacturer might have 30% of a regional market. However, when viewed on a national basis, the manufacturer might have only 3% of the total market for that good. This phenomenon may be a problem for many national companies that are not yet defining their market on a global basis. Their market positions depend a great deal on whether regional boundaries truly define product/market or competitive boundaries. To some degree, differences in cultures, languages, government policies, and costs may separate markets. However, one must be careful not to ignore possible competitive entry from foreign firms.

If a market definition is too broad, it is easy to gloss over meaningful differences in customer needs or competitive intentions. If the definition is too narrow, relative competitive position is likely to be overstated. The basic rule is that a market definition should be meaningful and present substantial competitive differences from related markets. If these differences do not exist, the relative market share measurement is essentially a misleading indicator of strategic position.

The Cash Sources/Uses Matrix

The cash sources/uses matrix can be used as a supplement to any portfolio analysis using the BCG growth/share matrix. One weakness of the BCG portfolio analysis is that there is little information on current product margins or fund allocation. The cash sources/uses matrix highlights this information based on planning assumptions by plotting a product's gross margin against its budget expenditures. As in the BCG analysis, the size of the circle plotted is based on sales volume in dollars. The vertical dividing line (left/right) represents average expenditures (advertising, promotion, etc.) per product, and the horizontal dividing line (top/bottom) represents average margin per product as a percent. A sample screen is shown in Exhibit 4.6.

Exhibit 4.6: Cash Sources/Uses Matrix

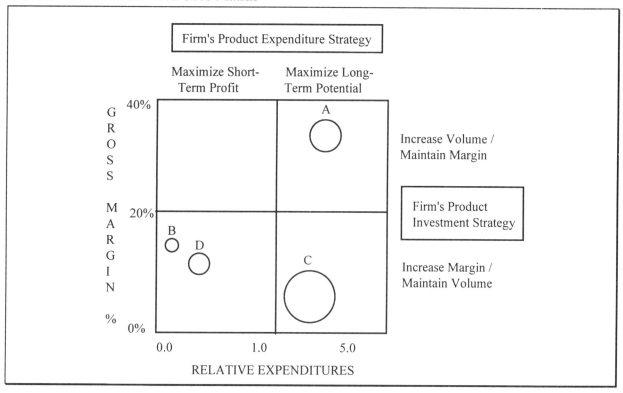

Products on the left side of the grid have been de-emphasized, in terms of budget expenditures, in your marketing portfolio. Some possible reasons may be external (the product requires less marketing support because it is in a smaller market, or that the market is less responsive to marketing mix variables), or they may be internal (you are attempting to milk the product, or other products have higher investment priorities). Those products on the right side receive higher percentages of the marketing budget. These products should have been chosen because of their greater long-term potential. Typically, these products should constitute a significant portion of firm sales (large circles), sell in high growth markets, or be central to your overall corporate strategy. Make sure that your reasoning on marketing emphasis (as defined by left/right positioning on this matrix) is consistent with your product strategy.

Products on the top half of the screen have higher than average margins. Each unit sold generates significant contribution (assuming similar price ranges). Therefore, your product strategy might focus on increasing units sold without sacrificing margins, possibly through the use of marketing variables or product improvements. The product strategy for those brands located in the lower half of the matrix should focus on reducing unit costs, thus increasing your unit margin. This is especially important for products that comprise a large portion of your company's sales.

When analyzing the example data it is clear that any reduction in costs for brand C will lead to a significant increase in profits. For instance, a 5% reduction in unit cost will result in an increased contribution of $7.9 million (172.5 x .92 x .05), or more than double the current contribution of $3.7 million. When factoring in the market growth, this becomes even more important. The strategy for brand A, on the other hand, might tend toward increasing sales because of the relatively high unit contribution generated by the brand. It is also apparent that brand D is receiving little support. Based on the BCG analysis, it may make sense to increase the support for this product because of the market growth, rather than pursuing a short-term milking strategy.

What then, should be concluded about the BCG growth/share analysis? First, that it is a simple method of evaluating alternative investment options for different product/markets. Second, unless further analysis is performed, its conclusions can be misleading and even dangerous. The cash sources/uses matrix can be used to augment the BCG matrix by also analyzing current margins and budget expenditures. However, other portfolio approaches have been developed to address some of the weaknesses in the BCG matrix. One such tool is the Industry Attractiveness-Business Position Matrix, first used at General Electric with help from the consulting firm of McKinsey & Company.

The Industry Attractiveness - Business Position Matrix

In this matrix, industry attractiveness and business position are substituted for market growth and relative share in the BCG model. Rather than limiting a market's attractiveness to one factor such as growth, or competitive position to relative share, this model allows for the combination of many factors on both axes. This model is based on the more generalized SWOT (Strengths/Weaknesses and Opportunities/Threats) analysis, where strengths and weaknesses make up competitive position while opportunities and threats determine industry attractiveness. The trade-off of this model is that many of these measures are more subjective and that the model is not as easy to implement quickly. The basic GE nine-cell matrix is displayed in Exhibit 4.7:

Exhibit 4.7: Industry Attractiveness - Business Position Matrix

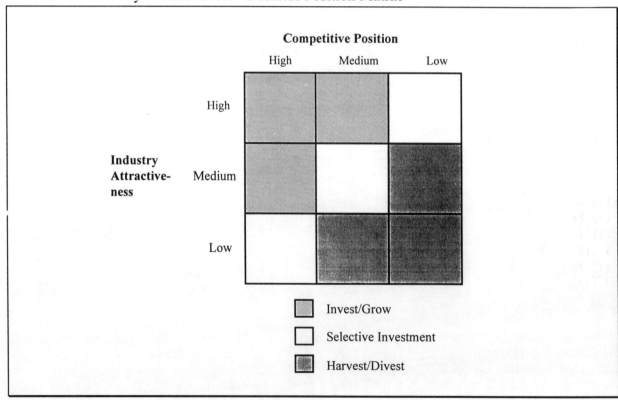

Each business is now evaluated on competitive position and long-term industry attractiveness. Some factors which could be used are suggested below:

Competitive Position	Industry Attractiveness
Relative market share	Growth rate
Competitive strengths and weaknesses	Profit margins
Market experience	Competitive rivalry
Management skill	Market size
Technological advantages	Emerging opportunities/threats
Distribution channels	Government/environmental issues
Customer base	Capital requirements

In the evaluation process, you may choose to include other factors or to ignore some of those listed above. The method of combining these factors should depend upon the situation for the SBU being assessed.

Once each SBU is plotted on the matrix, an analysis of investment alternatives should be made. Some of the usual alternatives include:

Invest   This may be to either gain share or to stop market share erosion. Typically, an increase in investment should only be made to SBUs that have a strong competitive position and are in an attractive industry. These are in the upper left corner of the matrix and should be considered strategic priorities.

Selective   Selective investment is made to SBUs that fall in the middle zone of the matrix. These are businesses where competitive position and industry attractiveness are both average, or one dimension is weak and the other strong. Often the appropriate investment level for these businesses is enough to hold/maintain current market position.

Withdraw   These are low investment priorities, and are located in the lower right corner of the matrix. Alternatives to pursue here are milking the business (attempting to generate cash with little investment) or selling the business.

One weakness of both the BCG and GE portfolio models is that neither addresses the need for new business investment. These models both analyze investment options within a current portfolio only. Therefore, one of the additional allocations of capital for either model should be in the new product/research area. It is essential that new SBUs (typically in high growth markets) are added to the portfolio along the way. Often these start as question marks in the BCG matrix. As time goes on, some of these new business opportunities may ultimately become stars through the use of appropriate strategic policies. Again, though, the key is achieving a reasonable balance within your portfolio.

Overall, portfolio analysis can add an important dimension to your strategic planning process. First, it can help companies better understand the dynamics shaping their businesses. Second, these models can offer some direction for investment priorities and the cash flow needs of various businesses. The BCG growth/share matrix is easy to implement, while the GE business matrix is a richer approach using multiple dimensions. Using the cash sources/uses matrix to highlight other issues such as average return on investment may enhance the information in these portfolio models. One should be careful not to rely solely on the outcomes from these models, but instead use them as a method of addressing portfolio goals and objectives to gain insights into the competitive position of a business.

There are two portfolio analysis forms located in the appendix for your use during the simulation. In period seven or eight, you should use the concepts introduced in this section in conjunction with the forms in the appendix or the PORTFOLIO GRAPH option under COMPANY. This will serve as the best method of applying the concepts of portfolio analysis.

Sources:

David A. Aaker, <u>Strategic Market Management</u>. John Wiley and Sons, 1984.

Bernhardt/Kinnear, <u>Cases in Marketing Management</u>. Business Publications Inc. 1988.

Bernhardt/Kinnear, <u>Principles of Marketing</u>, 3rd edition. Scott, Foresman, 1990.

Philip Kotler, <u>Marketing Management</u>, 5th edition. Prentice-Hall, 1984.

Roger W. Schmenner, <u>Production/Operations Management</u>, 2nd edition. SRA, 1984.

Thompson/Strickland, <u>Strategic Management</u>, 4th edition. BPI, 1987.

APPENDIX 1 - PharmaSim Glossary

Administrative Costs: Expenditures arising from the administration of a product, including some fixed overhead costs, some variable expenses, and some expenses related to the number of orders placed.

Advertising: Any paid form of non-personal presentation and promotion of ideas, goods, or services by an identified sponsor.

Advertising Message: The point that an advertisement is trying to make, whether to stimulate overall demand for a product group, stress the benefits of the product, compare with other brands, or maintain awareness.

Average Retail Price: The average price for a product charged by retailers, including both those stores with higher prices due to increased personal service, exclusive merchandise lines, attractive store atmosphere, special promotions, convenient location, or special services, and those who offer a no-frills, low-price approach.

BCG Growth-Share Matrix: A simplified view of marketing competition focusing on cash flow among businesses that was developed in the 1960s by the Boston Consulting Group. In the portfolio matrix, strategic business units (SBUs) are displayed on a two-dimensional grid. The horizontal axis gives market share relative to the industry's largest competitor, while the vertical axis represents the growth rate of the market. Positions of SBUs in the portfolio representing cash flow are signified as cash cows, dogs, question marks, and stars.

Brand Awareness: The level of consumer familiarity with a product, brand name, or promotional vehicle.

Brand Formulation: The physical structure or ingredients of a product or service.

Brand Image: The meaning consumers give to a product, based on the perceived benefits that the product provides.

Brand Loyalty: A favorable attitude toward, and exclusive purchase of, a brand over time.

Break-even Analysis: An attempt to determine the volume of sales necessary (at various prices) for the manufacturer or merchant to cover costs or to make revenue equal costs. Break-even analysis is useful to help set prices, estimate profit or loss potentials, and help determine the discretionary costs that should be incurred.

Cannibalization: Sales of a new product that decrease sales of another product in the product line.

Capacity Utilization: The extent to which the physical production ability of a plant facility is being used. Normally described as a percent of total capacity (i.e. 50% of capacity).

Channel of Distribution: Any firm or individual who participates in the flow of goods and services as they move from producer to ultimate user (consumer or industrial).

Cooperative (Co-op) Advertising: An agreement in which a manufacturer pays a portion of a retailer's local advertising costs.

Consumer Promotion: Sales promotion activities aimed at the consumer, including trial sizes of brands, coupons, and point-of-purchase displays.

Conversion Ratio: Of those consumers aware of a brand, the percent who have tried the brand (i.e. % trials / % aware).

Contribution After Marketing: The dollar amount remaining after total marketing expenditures are subtracted from the gross margin.

Cost of Goods Sold: The total variable manufacturing cost of producing a product.

Coupons: A promotional technique designed to convince consumers to purchase a product, by offering an individualized discount on the price of the item.

Demand: The desire of consumers for a certain product.

Demography: The study of people in the aggregate, including population size, age, income, occupation, and sex.

Detailers: Part of the indirect sales force that calls on doctors and pharmacists to provide information about their brand and to introduce new products. The objective is to have the doctor or pharmacists recommend their brand to the end consumer.

Direct Channel: Distribution flow of a product directly from manufacturer to retail outlet.

Direct Sales Force: Portion of sales force selling directly to retail outlets. The direct sales force is responsible for maintaining relationships with current retail accounts, developing new retail accounts, presenting trade promotions and allowances, and introducing new products to retailers.

Experience Curve Pricing: A price-setting method using a markup on the average total cost, as forecast by cost trends as sales volume accumulates.

Fixed Costs: Financial obligations of a firm that remain unchanged no matter how many units of a product are produced and marketed. Amortization charges for capital equipment and plant, plus such charges as rent, executive salaries, property taxes, and insurance are examples.

Geo-demographics: The neighborhood clustering of people with similar economic and cultural backgrounds and perspectives.

Gross Margin: Revenue less the cost of goods sold. (Price - unit cost) x units sold.

Income Statement: A report of a firm's overall results for a period, with a breakdown of major expenditures and a calculated value for the net income during the period.

Indirect Channel: Distribution channel from manufacturer to retail outlet by way of a wholesaler, merchandiser, or detailer.

Industry Attractiveness - Business Position Matrix: A business portfolio matrix dealing with factors besides market growth and relative share as shown in the BCG model. This nine-cell matrix allows for representation of a combination of factors along each axis.

Inflation: A general rise in the prices that people must pay for goods and services.

Line Extensions: The introduction of new flavors, sizes, or models into an existing product category, using an existing brand name.

Manufacturer Sales: Represents receipts from all sales, both direct and indirect, net of volume discounts.

Margin: The difference between the price of a product and its per unit cost.

Market: People or businesses with the potential interest, purchasing power, and willingness to spend money to buy a product or service that satisfies a need.

Market Penetration: The percentage of actual sales of a product category in relation to the total sales possible in a market.

Market Share: The percentage of sales of a certain product in a market in relation to other products in that market (i.e. Brand X / Total sales in market).

Marketing: The process of planning and executing the conception, pricing, promotion, and distribution of ideas, goods, and services to create exchanges that satisfy individual and organizational needs or wants.

Marketing Efficiency Index: The ratio of net income divided by marketing expenditures (advertising and promotion budget spent). This does not include promotional allowances, because it is viewed as a discount to the channel.

Marketing Research: The systematic and objective approach to the development and provision of information for marketing decision-making.

Markup Pricing: A price-setting method common in wholesaling and retailing, that adds a markup to average total or variable cost.

Mass Merchandisers: Very large retail stores that generally offer discount prices on items and have a high level of sales for products.

Media Type: The distinction between broad classes of media -- newspapers, magazines, television, radio, and so forth.

Merchandisers: Part of the indirect sales force that provides special support to retailers for in-store activities such as shelf location, pricing, and compliance with special programs.

Net Contribution: The contribution after marketing less fixed costs.

Net Income: The profit remaining after all costs are subtracted from revenues.

Point-of-Purchase Promotion (POP): Special displays, racks, signs, banners, and exhibits that are placed in the retail store to support the sales of a brand.

Portfolio Analysis: A way of classifying businesses or products, normally using the dimensions of market attractiveness (e.g. growth) and business position (e.g. relative market share).

Price: The amount of money a seller requires to provide goods or service to a customer.

Price Structure: The use of discounts, allowances, and freight cost absorption in determining price.

Primary Demand Stimulation: Advertising intended to affect demand for a whole product category, and not simply a specific brand.

Product Life-Cycle: The stages that a product class goes through during its time on the market, including introduction, growth, maturity, and decline.

Product Mix: All of the individual products available from an organization.

Promotion: The communication mechanism of marketing designed to inform and to persuade consumers to purchase.

Promotional Allowance: Reduction in the actual price paid by a channel member, resulting from an agreement to participate in promotional activity.

Purchase Intentions: What product or brand consumers intend to purchase before they actually enter the retail outlet to make the purchase.

Quality: The totality of features and characteristics of a product or service that bear on its ability to satisfy stated or implied needs.

Reformulations: Changes in the physical formulation of a brand to make the product more desirable to the consumer.

Reminder Advertising: A type of advertising message designed to maintain awareness and stimulate repurchase of an already established brand.

Research and Development Portion of a firm designated to research, analyze, and design products to meet consumer and market needs.

Retailer: A merchant whose main business is selling directly to the ultimate consumer for personal, non-business use.

Retention Ratio: The proportion of consumers who have tried a brand and repurchase the product.

Sales Force: Employees hired to promote and ultimately sell a manufacturer's product through either direct or indirect channels.

Segmentation: The process of dividing large heterogeneous markets into smaller homogeneous segments of people or businesses with similar needs and / or responsiveness to marketing mix offerings.

Sensitivity Analysis: Calculating the financial impact of various sales and cost scenarios, usually through "what if..." assumptions.

Share of Channel Sales: Market share segmented by the type of retail distribution outlet.

Shelf Space: The amount of space allocated to a product for display on retail store shelves. Shelf space often depends on the sales and profit potential of the product, as well as special arrangements between the store and manufacturer.

Shopping Habits: Consumer shopping preferences including product-type and retail channel preferences.

Strategic Business Unit (SBU): A unit within an organization that includes a distinct set of customers and competitors, has separate costs, and has the ability to undertake a separate strategy.

Trade Promotions: Sales promotion activities directed at wholesalers and retailers, including promotional allowances and cooperative advertising.

Trade Publications: Publications which are directed at a particular industry. Often these are generated by trade associations and contain articles of interest to the industry, as well as general market research and competitive information.

Unit Sales: The total volume of units sold by a manufacturer in a market.

Usage Rates: How often a product is used / purchased per year.

Variable Costs: Costs directly tied to production, including direct labor and raw materials charges.

Volume Discount: Reduction of list price based upon the quantity a buyer purchases. May be based upon a specific purchase (non-cumulative) or on total purchases over a period (cumulative).

Wholesale Price: A special discount price offered to wholesalers to encourage them to buy and sell merchandise in large quantities.

Wholesaler: A business unit that buys and resells merchandise to retailers, other merchants, and/or industrial, institutional, and commercial consumers.

Appendices 2 and 3 contain decision and planning forms for PharmaSim.

Any registered users may make additional photocopies of these forms for their own use when running the simulation.

APPENDIX 2 - PharmaSim Decision Forms (Level 1)

Period:

Item	Brands 1	2	3	Total
Brand Name				N/A
MSRP ($)				N/A
Promo Allowance (%)				N/A
Trade Promo ($)				
Consumer Promo ($)				
Advertising ($)				
Total Budget Spent				

	Direct (#)	Indirect (#)	Total (#)
Sales Force (# / Firm)			

Total = S + E + T	Salary ($)	Expenses ($)	Training($)	Total ($)
Sales Force Cost ($)				

Budget Spent = Promotion + Advertising + Sales Force + Reports

Total Budget Available		Total Budget Spent	

APPENDIX 2 - PharmaSim Decision Forms (Level 2)

Brand: **Period:**

Pricing:

MSRP($)	Discount Schedule (%)			
	<250	<2500	>2500	Wholesaler

Promotional Allowance (%):

Wholesale	Indep Drug	Chain Drug	Grocery	Conven	Mass Merch

Advertising:

Amount	$_____
Message	%Primary_____ %Benefits_____ %Compare_____ %Remind_____
Agency	BMW S&R LLC

Consumer and Trade Promotion:

	Co-op	P of P	Trial Size	Coupons
Amount ($)				

Sales Force Allocation (Firm):

Indep Drug	Chain Drug	Grocery	Conven	Mass Merch	Whole-saler	Merchan-disers	Detailer

APPENDIX 2 - PharmaSim Decision Forms (Level 3)

Brand: **Period:**

Pricing:

	Discount Schedule (%)			
MSRP($)	<250	<2500	>2500	Wholesaler

Promotional Allowance (%):

Wholesale	Indep Drug	Chain Drug	Grocery	Conven	Mass Merch

Advertising:

Amount ($)	%Primary_____	%Benefits_____	%Compare_____	%Remind_____	
Agency	BMW	S&R	LLC		
Target Segments	Singles Cold	Y. Fam Cough	M. Fam Allergy	Empty Nest	Retired
Brand Comparison	Brand Name_____				
Promote Benefits	Aches Allergy	Nasal No Side Eff.	Chest No Drows.	Runny Nose Rest	Cough

Consumer and Trade Promotion:

Amount($)	Indep Drug	Chain Drug	Grocery	Conven	Mass Merch
Co-op P of P					
Trial Size Coupons	Amount: 25¢	50¢	75¢	$1.00	

Sales Force Allocation (Firm):

Indep Drug	Chain Drug	Grocery	Conven	Mass Merch	Whole-saler	Merchan-disers	Detailer

APPENDIX 3 - PharmaSim Planning Forms

Firm Performance

Per.	Mfr's Sales		Market Share		Net Income		Other Measure	
	Obj	Res	Obj	Res	Obj	Res	Obj	Res
1								
2								
3								
4								
5								
6								
7								
8								
9								
10								

Obj = Planning Objective
Res = Actual Result

APPENDIX 3 - PharmaSim Planning Forms (Con't)

Brand Performance   **Brand:**

Per.	Mfr's Sales Obj	Mfr's Sales Res	Market Share Obj	Market Share Res	Brand Contribution Obj	Brand Contribution Res	Other Measure Obj	Other Measure Res
1								
2								
3								
4								
5								
6								
7								
8								
9								
10								

Obj = Planning Objective
Res = Actual Result

APPENDIX 3 - PharmaSim Planning Forms (Con't)

Marketing Plan   **Brand Name:**

Per.	Advertising ($) Obj	Advertising ($) Res	Trade Promo ($) Obj	Trade Promo ($) Res	Cons Promo ($) Obj	Cons Promo ($) Res	Sales Force ($) / Firm Obj	Sales Force ($) / Firm Res
1								
2								
3								
4								
5								
6								
7								
8								
9								
10								

Obj = Planning Objective
Res = Actual Result

APPENDIX 3 - PharmaSim Planning Forms (Con't)

BCG Portfolio Analysis   **Period:**

Brand	Brand Sales	Market Growth	Market Share	Compet. Mkt Share	Relative Mkt Share

Place each brand in the appropriate position on the BCG matrix based on market growth and relative market share. The size of the circle should correspond to the value of sales. What did you use as a definition of market for each brand?

High	Stars	?
Market Growth		
Low	Cash Cows	Dogs
	High	Rel Mkt Share	Low

APPENDIX 3 - PharmaSim Planning Forms (Con't)

GE Business Position / Industry Attractiveness   Period:

Brand	Business Position (High, Med, Low)	Industry Attractivenes (High, Med, Low)

Place each brand in the GE matrix below based on business (competitive) position and industry attractiveness. What factors did you use to arrive at your overall evaluation? What long-term strategy does your analysis suggest?

Competitive Position

		High	Medium	Low
Industry Attractive-ness	High			
	Medium			
	Low			

APPENDIX 3 - PharmaSim Planning Forms (Con't)

Strategic Objective(s):

Alternative Plans:

1.

2.

3.

Plan Choice / Reason:

Plan Implementation (Tactics):

APPENDIX 4 - Sample PharmaSim Market Survey Questionnaire

This market survey questionnaire was designed to be asked to consumers at the point of purchase (drugstore, grocery store, convenience store).

PURCHASE INFORMATION

1. Did you purchase any cold medicine?   Yes   No

   If NO, go to question 5.

2. Which brand of cold medicine did you purchase?   _____

PURCHASE INTENTIONS

3. Which brand of cold medicine did you intend to buy?   _____

SATISFACTION

4. Overall, are you satisfied with the product you just purchased?   Yes   No

BRAND AWARENESS

5. Which brands of cold medicine have you heard of?

Allround	Besthelp	Believe
Coldcure	Coughcure	Dripstop
Defogg	Effective	Extra
End	Other	

6. Which brands of cold medicine have you tried?

Allround	Besthelp	Believe
Coldcure	Coughcure	Dripstop
Defogg	Effective	Extra
End	Other	

7. Which brand of cold medicine do you purchase most frequently?

Allround	Besthelp	Believe
Coldcure	Coughcure	Dripstop
Defogg	Effective	Extra
End	Other	

DECISION CRITERIA

8. Please rank the following product attributes in order of importance in your decision to purchase cold medicine:

_____ Product Effectiveness

_____ Side Effects

_____ Price

_____ Form

_____ Duration

BRAND PERCEPTIONS/TRADEOFFS

9. Of the brands you mentioned you have heard of (from question 5),

How effective would you rate the _____ brand of cold medicine in relieving the following symptoms:

	Not at all effective			Extremely effective	
Aches	1	2	3	4	5
Nasal Congestion	1	2	3	4	5
Chest	1	2	3	4	5
Runny Nose	1	2	3	4	5
Cough	1	2	3	4	5
Allergy	1	2	3	4	5

What is your perception of the price of _____ brand?

	Inexpensive		Affordable		Expensive
Price	1	2	3	4	5

SEGMENT INFORMATION:

Age: _____

Household size: _____

What illness are you suffering from?   Cold   Cough   Allergy

APPENDIX 5 - Using PharmaSim in a Group

If you are using PharmaSim in a classroom setting, you may be asked by your professor to work in groups. Each group will pool their skills and resources to manage collectively as a brand manager, assistant brand manager, or brand assistant for over-the-counter cold medicines. Thus, your group will make specific decisions depending on the management position you are assigned.

Group work can be both rewarding and frustrating. However, it is the way business is most often conducted today. Thus, it's critical you learn how to make every group experience a success.

One of the most frequent complaints with group work is the amount of time wasted in trying to get organized and make decisions. There are also complaints that individual members are not "pulling their weight." To reduce these problems, your group should answer the following questions in their first meeting:

1. When, where, and how often should we meet?
2. How should we efficiently and effectively conduct our meetings?
3. Should we choose a general manager? What authority should this person have?
4. How should we divide the marketing tasks among group members?
5. How do we resolve marketing issues and make final decisions?
6. How do we encourage and maintain a high quality of contribution?
7. How will we deal with personal conflicts among group members?

Over time, the group should assess whether it is functioning efficiently and effectively. As your product portfolio changes, new competitive situations arise, and more information becomes available, the group may have to reorganize to best meet the current needs of the business.

APPENDIX 6 - PharmaSim Software Options and Trouble Shooting Guide

Win.ini Options

In the WIN.INI file, there are several options available which affect issues such as font choice, printer color and video display. The following entries represent the default values. The [PharmaSim] entry should be typed in just above the other options.

[PharmaSim]
display=color   (command to use a color printer)
propfont=fontname   (command to set the font for graphs, default is Arial)
fixedfont=courier new   (command to set the report font to fixed, courier font)
printer=displayfont   (command to set the print font to the display font, so that
                                          the printed image matches the screen)

Problems

The following is a list of some of the problems you might encounter when running PharmaSim, along with possible solutions. If an error message appears on the screen, please write it down. DBERR.$$$ files may also be created. These should not be deleted as they will provide clues as to the problem.

Problem: Cannot print graphs or printout is garbage.
Solution: Use the Control Panel command to select the correct printer.

Problem: Program stops with message "out of disk space".
Solution: There are too many files on your data disk. Try deleting unwanted files and restarting.

Problem: Assertion errors, database # errors.
Solution: Write down the description. Next time you start the simulation you will have the option of backup, restart, or cancel. Try REPLAY PERIOD, which will allow you to rerun the previous period. If that does not work, contact your instructor or Interpretive Software at (804) 979-0245. In most cases, we will be able to rebuild your database.

PharmaSim Index

Additional Blank Pages for Notes: